LIFE IN

Life in the Spirit

J. I. Packer

Hodder & Stoughton
LONDON SYDNEY AUCKLAND

Bible references are from the New International Version

Copyright © J. I. Packer 1996, an abridged edition
of *Through the Year with J. I. Packer*,
ed. Jean Watson, copyright © 1986

The right of J. I. Packer to be identified as
the author of this work has been asserted by him
in accordance with the
Copyright, Designs and Patents Act 1988.

10 9 8 7 6 5 4 3 2 1

All rights reserved.
No part of this publication may be reproduced,
stored in a retrieval system, or transmitted,
in any form or by any means,
without the prior written permission of the publisher,
nor be otherwise circulated in any form of binding or cover
other than that in which it is published and without a
similar condition being imposed on the subsequent purchaser.

A CIP catalogue record for this title is available
from the British Library.

ISBN 0 340 64174 6

Typeset by Hewer Text Composition Services, Edinburgh
Printed and bound in Great Britain by
Cox & Wyman, Reading, Berks

Hodder and Stoughton Ltd
A division of Hodder Headline PLC
338 Euston Road
London NW1 3BH

Contents

	Preface	7
	Life from the Spirit	
1	New birth	11
2	New life	14
3	Inner assurance	17
4	New sources of joy	20
5	Ongoing salvation	24
	Spiritual growth	
6	True wisdom	31
7	Love in the Spirit	35
8	Willing service	38
9	Ongoing struggles	42
10	Still under construction	45
	Taught by the Spirit	
11	Reality in focus	51
12	Inspired truth	54
13	The unity of Scripture	58
14	Receptive to truth	62
15	Praying in the Spirit	66
	Effective through the Spirit	
16	Not grieving but filled	71
17	Ready for battle	75
18	Prayer – how?	79
19	Prayer – for what?	82
20	Prayer – for whom?	85

One in the Spirit

21	Wholehearted worship	91
22	Healthy unity	94
23	Genuine fellowship	97
24	Spiritual gifts	101
25	Spiritual graces	105

Experiencing the Spirit

26	Focus on Jesus	111
27	Guidance and guidelines	114
28	Spiritual authority	118
29	Spiritual movements	122
30	All this and heaven too!	126

Notes	129
Bibliography	135
For Further Notes	137

Preface

Life in the Spirit is a daily devotional in the *20 Minutes with God* series. It has been brought to birth by the spectacular midwifery of Jean Watson, drawing on material she once put into shape in a book that bore the ominous title *Through the Year with J. I. Packer*. I think she has done a brilliant job; I hope that you who use this book will agree.

The publishers and I believe that *Life in the Spirit* is equally suited for both personal and group use. In either case, however, please note that what is offered here is meant only to set you going. It has the nature of a starting block rather than a finishing post. If this material primes the pump of your heart I shall be thankful, but that is all I can properly hope for it to do. God the Holy Spirit himself, the true author, authenticator and interpreter of Scripture, must lead you directly as you seek to make connections between the Word of God and your own life. The pieces of Packer that are set out here to help you read, mark, learn and inwardly digest the message of Scripture will, I hope, tune you in to the Spirit's leading. My prayer is that all who use *Life in the Spirit* will find themselves Spirit-led in this deep applicatory way.

So I here repeat what I wrote on another occasion: these droppings from my head and heart should be your starting-point, not your resting-place. Use them as a springboard or trampoline before the Lord. Bounce on

8   *LIFE IN THE SPIRIT*   □

them, bounce off them, and see how high your heavenly Father enables you to go.

J. I. Packer

Life from the Spirit

1

New birth

Reading: Ephesians 2:1–10

As for you, you were dead in your transgressions and sins, in which you used to live when you followed the ways of this world and of the ruler of the kingdom of the air, the spirit who is now at work in those who are disobedient. All of us also lived among them at one time, gratifying the cravings of our sinful nature and following its desires and thoughts. Like the rest, we were by nature objects of wrath. But because of his great love for us, God, who is rich in mercy, made us alive even when we were dead in transgressions – it is by grace you have been saved. And God raised us up with Christ and seated us with him in the heavenly realms in Christ Jesus, in order that in the coming ages he might show the incomparable riches of his grace, expressed in his kindness to us in Christ Jesus. For it is by grace you have been saved, through faith – and this not from yourselves, it is the gift of God – not by works, so that no one can boast. For we are God's workmanship, created in Christ Jesus to do good works, which God prepared in advance for us to do.

12   *LIFE IN THE SPIRIT*   □

Paul speaks clearly in our reading and elsewhere of the new birth as the act of God by which those who were spiritually dead are made alive in Christ.

When he describes people as being spiritually dead, he means that they are unresponsive to God (corpses don't answer when you address them); they are separated from God's fellowship and exposed to God's wrath. Such people follow a course of life dictated by the world, the devil, and the flesh – a life of disobedience to God.

Concerning God's quickening of the spiritually dead, Paul points out:

- it springs from *love*, *mercy*, *grace*, and *kindness* so completely that it is largely beyond our thought;
- it takes place *in Christ*. Jesus Christ is the mediator of all God's gifts to us, including newness of life;
- it catches us up into God's act of *raising Christ from the dead*. The church is the extension of the resurrection. Those raised with Christ sit in the heavenlies: they enjoy a hidden life which puts them always 'on top' since he who is ruling the world makes all things work for their good.

A course of *God-planned obedience* is its goal.[1]

What actually happens through the new birth is an inner recreating of fallen human nature by the Holy Spirit. Regeneration changes the disposition from lawless, godless self-seeking into one of trust and love, of repentance for past rebelliousness and unbelief, and loving compliance with God's law henceforth. It enlightens the blinded mind to discern spiritual realities and liberates and energises the enslaved will for free obedience to God.

The use of the figure of new birth to describe this change emphasises two facts about it. The first is its decisiveness. The regenerate man has forever ceased to be the man he was; his old life is over and a new life has begun; he is a new creature in Christ, buried with him out of reach of condemnation and raised with him into a new life of righteousness.

The second fact emphasised is that regeneration is due to the free and, to us, mysterious, exercise of divine power. Infants do not induce or co-operate in their own procreation and birth; no more can those who are dead in trespasses and sins prompt the quickening operation of God's Spirit within them.[2]

Reflection

Can you identify some of the things that have changed or are changing in your life as a result of your spiritual rebirth?

Take time to thank God for these. Then, if appropriate, think and pray about disappointments (with him, with yourself, or both) in this area.

2
New life

Reading: Galatians 5:16–24

So I say, live by the Spirit, and you will not gratify the desires of the sinful nature. For the sinful nature desires what is contrary to the Spirit, and the Spirit what is contrary to the sinful nature. They are in conflict with each other, so that you do not do what you want. But if you are led by the Spirit, you are not under law.

The acts of the sinful nature are obvious: sexual immorality, impurity and debauchery; idolatry and witchcraft; hatred, discord, jealousy, fits of rage, selfish ambition, dissensions, factions and envy; drunkenness, orgies and the like. I warn you, as I did before, that those who live like this will not inherit the kingdom of God.

But the fruit of the Spirit is love, joy, peace, patience, kindness, goodness, faithfulness, gentleness and self-control. Against such things there is no law. Those who belong to Christ have crucified the sinful nature with its passions and desires.

It is by the Spirit's enabling that Christians resolve to do particular things that are right, and actually do them, and

NEW LIFE

thus form habits of doing right things; and out of these habits comes a character that is right.

What are the means which the Spirit uses? He uses the objective means of grace (biblical truth, prayer, fellowship, worship, and the Lord's Supper) and the subjective means of grace whereby we open ourselves to change (thinking, listening, questioning, admonishing and examining ourselves, sharing what is in our heart with others, and weighing any response they make). These are the Spirit's ordinary ways of leading us on in holiness. I believe visions, impressions, and prophecies come only rarely and to some believers not at all.

From one standpoint, the fruit of the Spirit is a series of habits formed by action and reaction. Love, joy, peace, patience, kindness, goodness, faithfulness, gentleness, self-control are all habitual dispositions: that is, accustomed ways of thinking, feeling, and behaving. We must remember, however, that these habits, though formed in a natural manner by self-discipline and effort, are not natural products. The discipline and effort must be blessed by the Holy Spirit or they would achieve nothing. So all our attempts to get our lives into shape need to be soaked in constant, humble, thankful prayer.[1]

It is very important that we remove from our minds any conceited notion which suggests that as we grow in holiness we shall need the cleansing blood of Christ less. We shall never get beyond our need for the blood of Jesus. The context of our sanctification is justification by the blood of Christ.

The source of our sanctification is union with Christ. We are united with him at the point where our first life (our old life) ends and the new life begins. The beginning of the new life means the renewing of our hearts so that now we love God and his will, ways, and purposes, and discover our deepest desire – to know, love, get and keep close to, serve, please, and praise him all our days. The summons to be holy is simply the call to be natural as a Christian and let those new instincts, impulses, and longings express themselves in the way we live.

The agent of sanctification is the Holy Spirit who works in us to make us will and act according to God's good pleasure. Again and again we need to go down on our knees and admit our helplessness and ask to be empowered. Then, believing that God has heard and answered us, we need to move into action, attempting to do the very thing about which we have prayed.

If all this sounds easy, it shouldn't, because sanctification is a battle. We never have our hearts entirely set on the things of God, so that even if our actions are right by external standards, our hearts are never quite right. It is struggle and conflict all the way.[2]

Reflection

Pray: 'Teach me how to grow in goodness.' This is a good prayer, but how is such a prayer answered?

Philippians 2:12 urges us to work out what God works in. Can you clarify, from the reading and comments and also, if you have time, from Ephesians 4:22–32, what God has done and continues to do for us and what we have to do in response to that in order to grow in goodness?

3

Inner assurance

Reading: Romans 8:15–17

You did not receive a spirit that makes you a slave again to fear, but you received the Spirit of sonship. And by him we cry, 'Abba, Father.' The Spirit himself testifies with our spirit that we are God's children. Now if we are children, then we are heirs – heirs of God and co-heirs with Christ, if indeed we share in his sufferings in order that we may also share in his glory.

We are reconciled to God through the death of his Son. This death redeems us and redemption carries the idea of liberation through the payment of a price. Jesus' death for our sins also defeated Satan. Paul speaks vividly of Christ conquering the devil and his hosts, shaking off the principalities and powers, triumphing publicly over them in the manner of a general leading a procession of prisoners and spoils after a victorious campaign – and all this, Paul tells us, happened on the cross. So God saves first of all by the event

18   *LIFE IN THE SPIRIT*   □

of the cross and symbolises his victory in the resurrection.

Secondly, God saves by the continuing ministry of Christ who finds and keeps those for whom he died, brings them into grace, calls them into faith, intercedes for them so that they find grace to help in time of need, protects them when world, flesh, and devil attack them, and finally transforms them into his likeness. He shall change the body of our lowly state so as to fashion it like his glorious body, says Paul. That is part of the Christian hope: a body to match one's already renewed spirit.

Thirdly, God saves us by the ministry of the Holy Spirit whom the saved receive as God's seal set upon them to mark them as his and to bring them in experience the first instalment of the salvation which is finally to be theirs with Christ in glory.[1]

Christians may be tempted to doubt these truths; to fear that fellowship with God will be broken because of their weak and wobbly, up-and-down sort of Christian lives. But Paul answers that fear by pointing out that we have been adopted for all eternity into God's family and that God's Spirit within us is constantly assuring us that we are God's children. This assurance takes the form not so much of an arresting feeling as of a filial instinct and a sustained confidence, as our reading makes clear.

It is the Spirit's work to keep the Christian aware that as a forgiven sinner he has become God's child, that his life must be lived out of that adoptive relationship, and that his hope of glory is precisely the prospect of inheriting his father's riches. God has made us joint heirs with Christ, destined to share all the glory and joy that is his, and he will not go back on that; so we need not fear that the uneven quality of our Christian lives will rob us of our present standing in God's favour. It is heaven on earth to find oneself unable to doubt that this is so – and that is the essence of the God-given spirit of sonship.[2]

Reflection

Is there a gap between how assured you in fact are and how assured you feel? Meditate in the Spirit's presence on the ground and content of your spiritual assurance. You might find it helpful to put your thoughts onto paper briefly, e.g. Because of . . .

. . . I am assured about . . .

Pray that the Spirit will testify with your spirit – give you an inner sense of assurance – as to all that you can feel secure and confident about.

4

New sources of joy

Reading: Romans 5:1–11

Therefore, since we have been justified through faith, we have peace with God through our Lord Jesus Christ, through whom we have gained access by faith into this grace in which we now stand. And we rejoice in the hope of the glory of God. Not only so, but we also rejoice in our sufferings, because we know that suffering produces perseverance; perseverance, character; and character, hope. And hope does not disappoint us because God has poured out his love into our hearts by the Holy Spirit, whom he has given us.

You see, at just the right time, when we were still powerless, Christ died for the ungodly. Very rarely will anyone die for a righteous man, though for a good man someone might possibly dare to die. But God demonstrates his own love for us in this: while we were still sinners, Christ died for us.

Since we have now been justified by his blood, how much more shall we be saved from God's wrath through him! For if, when we were enemies, we were reconciled to him through the death of his Son, how much more, having been reconciled, shall we be saved through his life! Not only is this so, but we also rejoice in God through our Lord Jesus Christ, through whom we have now received reconciliation.

To know that you are loved – that is one source of joy. No one has joy who does not know that there is someone who values him, cares for him, accepts him. To feel that nobody cares for me, treats me as a person, or bothers with me, and that I matter to nobody is a great joy-killer. Now the Christian knows love in a way that nobody else does, for he knows that God so loved the world that he gave his only Son to die in shame for us on the cross, that we who believe in him might have eternal life. The measure of God's love to us is how much he gave for us. To know that Christ 'loved me and gave himself for me' is to realise divine love in a way that brings endless joy. God cares for me! He redeemed me!

Discontent is another great joy-killer, whereas to accept our situation is a source of joy. Now Christians can always do that because they know that all their circumstances are planned out for them by a loving heavenly Father. Speaking from prison with the death sentence hanging over him, Paul wrote: 'I have learned to be content whatever the circumstances' (Phil. 4:11).

Joy comes too from an awareness that we have something worth having. People say, 'My spouse, children, home, books, hobbies, and so on are a joy to me.' But Paul speaks of 'the surpassing greatness of knowing Christ Jesus my Lord' (Phil. 3:8). With Paul, the Christian says: 'I have Jesus, the pearl of great price. I will let anything go in order to hold on to him and enjoy him fully.'[1]

Another source of joy is the knowledge that you are giving something worth giving; a belief that you have significance for others because of what you have to impart to them. Giving is a supreme source of joy. If you have something that is supremely worth giving, you will find joy in trying to share it even when you feel sorrow that the gift is not being accepted. Paul knew that joy, for Paul gave himself, his whole life, to bring light into people's sin-darkened lives by sharing with them the blessings of the gospel. Like him, we will find joy in passing on God's best gift.

Once we know the sources of spiritual joy, we need to choose it. That is what the command to rejoice in the Lord requires of us. How do we choose joy? By practising the art of Christian thinking. By choosing to dwell, over and over again, on our source of joy, saying to ourselves and perhaps to others also: Yes, he loves and accepts me. Yes, my circumstances are sent by God for my good. Yes, I have something supremely worth having: the knowledge of my Saviour. Yes, I am doing something supremely worth doing in seeking every opportunity to share Jesus Christ with others. As we think over these things, joy wells up spontaneously. You choose joy, you see, by directing your thoughts to that which triggers it.

Jesus wants our joy to be full and has made abundant provision for its fullness. Once we learn the art of Christian thinking, streams of joy will flow out into our hearts every day of our lives. This is one aspect of the victory that overcomes the world, even our faith, from which comes the joy which no man can quench and which gives us strength for service we never knew we had.[2]

Reflection

List the sources of joy mentioned in the reading and the comments.

NEW SOURCES OF JOY

Underline those you can identify with and add other sources of joy in your life not on the list.

Making and regularly updating a joy-list can be one way of bringing about positive attitude changes. How about trying it?

5

Ongoing salvation

Reading: Titus 3:3–7

At one time we too were foolish, disobedient, deceived and enslaved by all kinds of passions and pleasures. We lived in malice and envy, being hated and hating one another. But when the kindness and love of God our Saviour appeared, he saved us, not because of righteous things we had done, but because of his mercy. He saved us through the washing of rebirth and renewal by the Holy Spirit, whom he poured out on us generously through Jesus Christ our Saviour, so that, having been justified by his grace, we might become heirs having the hope of eternal life.

If we are Christians, we *have been* saved as God's gift of justification has saved us from sin's *penalty*; we *are being* saved as we are kept daily from falling under sin's *power*; and we *will be* fully and finally saved when we are freed from sin's *presence* and from all its traces at Christ's coming. These are the three aspects of our salvation; and there are three means by which we are saved.

ONGOING SALVATION

First, the sacrificial death of Christ was the means whereby God provided salvation. He gave his life as ransom for many, shedding his blood, like that of a lamb without blemish or spot, for the remission of our sins.

Second, faith alone, apart from works, is the means whereby we receive salvation. Faith is an outgoing of the soul in belief and commitment toward a threefold object: the God of the Bible; the Christ of God, who is the Christ of the Bible; and the teaching and promises of God, which are the teachings and promises of the Bible. Faith receives the truth of God and trusts the person – or rather, the three persons – of God. Repentance, which means turning or changing one's mind, is the negative side of faith. It is saying 'No' to the old godless ways in order to say 'Yes' to Christ henceforth.

Third, regeneration by the Holy Spirit is the means whereby God conveys salvation. As Jesus told Nicodemus, a person cannot see or enter the kingdom of God (the realm of salvation) without being born again. The word 'cannot' reveals that fallen human beings like ourselves lack the power to turn to God and exercise faith unless the Holy Spirit works in our hearts.[1]

The Holy Spirit plays a vital part too in our ongoing salvation. In the New Testament he is set forth as the third divine person, linked with and yet distinct from the Father and the Son, just as the Father and the Son are distinct from each other. He is the *paraclete* – a rich word for which there is no adequate English translation since it means by turns comforter (strengthener), counsellor, helper, supporter, adviser, advocate, ally, senior friend – and only a person could fulfil such roles. More precisely he is another paraclete, second in line (we may say) to the Lord Jesus, continuing Jesus' own ministry – and only a person, one like Jesus, could do that.

John underlines the point by repeatedly using a masculine pronoun to render Jesus' reference to the Spirit, when Greek grammar called for a neuter one to agree with the neuter noun 'Spirit'. John wants his readers to be in no doubt that the Spirit is *he* not *it*.

Again the Holy Spirit is said to hear, speak, witness, convince, glorify Christ, lead, guide, teach, command, forbid, desire, give speech, give help, and intercede for Christians with inarticulate groans, himself crying to God in their prayers. Also he can be lied to and grieved. Such things could only be said of a person. The conclusion is that the Spirit is not just an influence; he, like the Father and the Son, is an individual person.[2]

Reflection

Put into your own words the part played by the three persons in the Trinity in effecting our ongoing salvation.

The whole Trinity involved in my salvation – mind-blowing! Does this thought prompt you to dance, sing, write a poem to express your joy and give thanks?

For further study
The Holy Spirit as a divine person – the following passages

might start you off on a study of this theme: John 14:16–17, 25–26; 16:7–15; Acts 2:4; 5:3,4; 8:29; 13:2; 16:6–7; Romans 8:5–27; 1 Corinthians 2:14; Galatians 4:6–7; 5:16–26; Ephesians 4:30.

Spiritual growth

6

True wisdom

Reading: James 3:13–18

Who is wise and understanding among you? Let him show it by his good life, by deeds done in the humility that comes from wisdom. But if you harbour bitter envy and selfish ambition in your hearts, do not boast about it or deny the truth. Such 'wisdom' does not come down from heaven but is earthly, unspiritual, of the devil. For where you have envy and selfish ambition, there you find disorder and every evil practice.

But the wisdom that comes from heaven is first of all pure; then peace-loving, considerate, submissive, full of mercy and good fruit, impartial and sincere. Peacemakers who sow in peace raise a harvest of righteousness.

Wisdom in the Bible embraces the thought of discerning the best thing to aim at and being able to choose the best means to that end. Jesus chose the best thing to aim at – namely his Father's will: that he should redeem men and women and bring a multitude of sinners to glory. Then he chose the best means to that end. His Father taught him from the Old Testament Scriptures what sort of person the Messiah, God's appointed Saviour, must be. Jesus understood this; he knew that the way to his kingdom was via the cross and he went that way. This was an expression of his wisdom.

His wisdom was also shown in his teaching and in his dealings with people. Because he knew and understood what was wisdom for his own life, he was able to help others to know and understand wisdom in their own lives. It's generally true that one who understands how to follow God's will for his or her life is able to guide another person in this area. God's will for others won't necessarily be identical to God's will for me, but having worked out the next step of the way that God wants me to go, I can share the principles which will help others to find the overall strategy and the next step that is right for them.

Look at Jesus, then, as embodying the perfection of God's wisdom. This is one aspect of the total human maturity (emotional and ethical) which Jesus showed and which the Holy Spirit starts to bring about in us.[1]

What steps must a man or woman take to lay hold of the gift of wisdom? There are two prerequisites according to Scripture.

First, one must learn to *reverence God*. 'The fear of the LORD is the beginning of wisdom' (Ps. 111:10). Not until we have become humble and teachable, standing in awe of God's holiness and sovereignty, acknowledging our own littleness, distrusting our own thoughts, and willing to have our minds turned upside down, can divine wisdom become ours. It is to be feared that many Christians spend all their lives in too unhumbled and conceited a frame of mind ever to gain wisdom from God at all. Scripture says: 'With humility comes wisdom' (Prov. 11:2).

Then one must learn to *receive God's Word*. Wisdom is divinely wrought in those, and those only, who apply themselves to God's revelation. 'I have more insight than all my teachers' – why? – *'for I meditate on your statutes'* (Ps. 119:99). So Paul admonishes the Colossians: 'Let *the word of Christ* dwell in you richly, as you teach and admonish one another with all wisdom' (Col. 3:16).

How are we to do this? By soaking ourselves in the Scriptures, which, as Paul told Timothy (and he had in mind the Old Testament alone!), 'are able to make you wise for salvation through faith in Christ', and to perfect the man of God 'for every good work' (2 Tim. 3:15–17).[2]

Reflection

Ask the Holy Spirit to help you to become aware both of your wisdom-friendly and of your anti-wisdom attitudes and characteristics as identified below, based on the reading.

Anti-wisdom
bitterness
envy
selfishness
disorder

Wisdom-friendly
peace-loving
considerate
submissive
merciful
good
impartial
sincere

34   *LIFE IN THE SPIRIT*   □

For further Bible study
Use a concordance to find and study passages that have
something to say about spiritual wisdom and maturity:
what it is, how it is expressed (in character, lifestyle, etc)
and how we can aim for and start to attain it. These references might start you off: Psalm 19:7; 51:6; 111:10; Luke
2:52; 8:14; Galatians 5:22; Ephesians 4:10–13; Philippians
3:12–16; 2 Timothy 3:10–17.

7

Love in the Spirit

Reading: 1 Corinthians 13:1–8

If I speak in the tongues of men and of angels, but have not love, I am only a resounding gong or a clanging cymbal. If I have the gift of prophecy and can fathom all mysteries and all knowledge, and if I have a faith that can move mountains, but have not love, I am nothing. If I give all I possess to the poor and surrender my body to the flames, but have not love, I gain nothing.

Love is patient, love is kind. It does not envy, it does not boast, it is not proud. It is not rude, it is not self-seeking, it is not easily angered, it keeps no record of wrongs. Love does not delight in evil but rejoices with the truth. It always protects, always trusts, always hopes, always perseveres.

Love never fails.

Love in the Spirit is surely gratitude to God and goodwill towards men in response to knowing the love of the Father, who gave the Son, and of the Son, who gave himself for our salvation.

Modelling itself on this divine love, love in the Spirit becomes a habit of self-giving service in which some element of a person's life is constantly being laid down for someone else's sake. Paul draws its profile in our reading. It has as its heart an ongoing altruism, a desire to see others made great, good, holy, and happy – a passion that this fallen world finds incomprehensible and which in itself is altogether supernatural.[1]

The Greek word *agape* (love) seems to have been virtually a Christian invention – a new word for a new thing (apart from about twenty occurrences in the Greek version of the Old Testament, it is almost non-existent before the New Testament). *Agape* draws its meaning directly from the revelation of God in Christ. It is not a form of natural affection, however intense, but a supernatural fruit of the Spirit. It is a matter of will rather than feeling (for Christians must love even those they dislike). It is the basic element in Christlikeness.

Note what the reading has to say about the primacy and permanence of love; note too the profile of love which it gives.

Tongues, prophetic gifts, theological expertise, and miracle-working faith preoccupied the Corinthians; giving everything away and accepting martyrdom may be required of Christians at any time. Yet love matters so much more than these things that without it they all become worthless, and the loveless Christian, however gifted and active, gains nothing and is nothing.

These verses give us a portrait of Jesus and correct the bumptious, contentious, suspicious, presumptuous, arrogant, self-assertive, critical, irresponsible spirit of the Corinthians that made Paul have to call them carnal and spiritually babyish.

The greater importance of love appears from the fact that it will last through the life to come when all occasion for tongues, prophecy, and theological instruction will have ceased.[2]

Reflection

Under either of the headings below, list the aspects of love mentioned in the reading. Then, opposite every 'Love is' positive quality put the contrasting negative quality, under the 'Love is not' heading, and vice versa.

Love is . . .   *Love is not . . .*

Underline anything that is particularly significant for you – because of a fraught relationship or an area of fear in your life, for example.

Keep asking God for, and keep being ready to receive, whatever aspects of love in the Spirit you particularly need.

8

Willing service

Reading: Philippians 2:1–7

If you have any encouragement from being united with Christ, if any comfort from his love, if any fellowship with the Spirit, if any tenderness and compassion, then make my joy complete by being like-minded, having the same love, being one in spirit and purpose. Do nothing out of selfish ambition or vain conceit, but in humility consider others better than yourselves. Each of you should look not only to your own interests, but also to the interests of others.

Your attitude should be the same as that of Christ Jesus:

Who, being in very nature God,
 did not consider equality with God something to be
  grasped,
 but made himself nothing,
 taking the very nature of a servant,
 being made in human likeness.

WILLING SERVICE

39

As an outcrop and sample of the church universal, created in Christ by the Holy Spirit of God, the local church has its own proper life to live – a life lived on very different principles and for very different ends from the life of the world around. The church's life, we are told, must be one of *love* – a life of gratitude to God in which we seek to imitate our Saviour by love towards all people, and particularly those who are both his brothers and sisters and ours.

Specifically, this life of love is to be a life of *fellowship* whereby we share (for that is what fellowship really means) the good things that God has given us individually. No Christian is self-sufficient; we all need each other and what God has given each other; we must learn, therefore, to express our love in the give-and-take of Christian fellowship. And this loving fellowship must take the form of *ministry* (*diakonia*, in Greek; service, in literal English). 'Serve one another in love' (Gal. 5:13). In this basic sense the church's ministry is a vocation to which every Christian is called.

It is for this life of ministry, in which every part of the body is called to make its contribution, that God gives *gifts*. Gifts and ministry are in this sense correlative; God gives each man his gift not primarily for himself but for others to be used for their good in the fellowship of the body's life.[1]

The 'servant' image is relevant in this context. It denotes a man who is not at his own disposal, but is his master's purchased property. Bought to serve his master's needs, to be at his beck and call every moment, the slave's sole business is to do as he is told. And Christian service means living out a slave-relationship to one's Saviour.

What work does Christ set his servants to do? The way that they serve him, he tells them, is by becoming the slaves of their fellow-servants and being willing to do literally anything, however costly, irksome, or undignified, in order to help them. This is what love means, as he himself showed at the Last Supper when he played the slave's part and washed the disciples' feet.

When the New Testament speaks of ministering to the saints, it means not primarily preaching to them but devoting time, trouble, and substance to giving them all the practical help possible. The essence of Christian service is loyalty to the king expressing itself in care for his servants.

Only the Holy Spirit can create in us the kind of love towards our Saviour that will overflow in imaginative sympathy and practical helpfulness towards his people. Unless the Spirit is training us in love, we are not fit persons to go to college or a training class to learn the know-how of particular branches of Christian work. Gifted leaders who are self-centred and loveless are a blight in the church rather than a blessing.[2]

Reflection

To what extent are you involved in contributing something which others enjoy or need and in receiving from others something which you enjoy or need?

Which do you find harder – contributing or receiving/identifying what you contribute or what you receive? What does this tell you about yourself? Is there food for thought, prayer or other action here?

9

Ongoing struggles

Reading: Romans 8:22–25

We know that the whole creation has been groaning as in the pains of childbirth right up to the present time. Not only so, but we ourselves, who have the firstfruits of the Spirit, groan inwardly as we wait eagerly for our adoption as sons, the redemption of our bodies. For in this hope we were saved. But hope that is seen is no hope at all. Who hopes for what he already has? But if we hope for what we do not yet have, we wait for it patiently.

What do Christians groan inwardly about? They groan about the fact that their bodies (meaning their total personal selves) are still the seat of indwelling sin; the old anti-God instincts and urges are still *resident*, although not *dominant*. As fallen beings, all our physical and mental desires are naturally inclined to be inordinate, disorderly, and uncontrolled. Gluttony is one form of inordinate desire which is a problem for some. Others may selfishly exploit their fellows out of an inordinate

ONGOING STRUGGLES

longing for advancement and success. Desires become inordinate in all sorts of ways because of the kinds of persons that we are in these unredeemed bodies of ours. Inordinate desires are constantly seeking to lead us astray and so there is constant tension in the Christian life.

The believer, who from her heart delights in the law of God, also finds another principle operating in herself: a law warring against the law of her mind and inclining her to all sorts of disobedience and self-indulgence. She starts each day saying, 'Lord, let it be all right today,' and ends it admitting, 'Lord, it hasn't all been right today.' As long as she is in the body indwelling sin is still with her, much as she wishes it wasn't.[1]

It is easy to despair of ever making headway against moral weaknesses that have ensnared us again and again. But by praying for the Spirit's help to watch against them, especially in times of temptation, and by letting the Spirit lead us to love Christ more so that we love sin less, we may drain the life and energy out of these ugly habits.

There's an old story about a missionary and an ex-cannibal who had become a Christian. His grandfather had been a cannibal of distinction and a wild man in other ways, and the missionary told him to think of his own continuing impulses to sin as grandfather in his bones. After some years of furlough, the missionary returned and asked him, 'How is grandfather in your bones these days?'

'He's still alive,' came the reply, 'but he don't get around like he used to!'

Every Christian's experience ought to be like that. Sin is still in us and the war is not yet over, but we may win victories over it constantly and weaken its power and allure as we follow the Spirit's prompting to look to the Lord and say no to the temptation. As when, trusting the Lord, we resist the devil we find that he flees, so when, still trusting the Lord, we resist each temptation we find that it retreats, and attacks less strongly as time goes by. Have you not found this already? It is your privilege to prove it, starting today. The crucial question is: are you willing to see your beloved sins die in this way?[2]

Our physical dispositions and states may also give us all sorts of difficulties to contend with. Some are saddled with depressive temperaments, or fiery tempers, or butterfly minds, or extreme shyness; menopausal tensions are acute for some, and all of us have to cope with coming apart at the seams in old age. These factors constantly occasion sin and obstruct righteousness. They, too, merit our groans.

Reflection

Use Romans chapters 7 and 8 and your own past and present experience to help you make notes under the headings below.

Sources of struggle and groaning: Sources of joy and victory:

Underline in both columns what you can particularly identify with at present. Focus on and try to take with you into the day the words and thoughts that could encourage and strengthen you as you go about your life and work.

10

Still under construction

Reading: Ephesians 2:13–22

Now in Christ Jesus you who once were far away have been brought near through the blood of Christ.

For he himself is our peace, who has made the two one and has destroyed the barrier, the dividing wall of hostility, by abolishing in his flesh the law with its commandments and regulations. His purpose was to create in himself one new man out of the two, thus making peace, and in this one body to reconcile both of them to God through the cross, by which he put to death their hostility. He came and preached peace to you who were far away and peace to those who were near. For through him we both have access to the Father by one Spirit.

Consequently, you are no longer foreigners and aliens, but fellow-citizens with God's people and members of God's household, built on the foundation of the apostles and prophets, with Christ Jesus himself as the chief cornerstone. In him the whole building is joined together and rises to become a holy temple in the Lord. And in him you too are being built together to become a dwelling in which God lives by his Spirit.

When Christ came, the Old Testament concept of the church was not destroyed but fulfilled. Christ, the mediator of the covenant, was the link between the Mosaic and the Christian dispensations. The New Testament depicts him as the true Israel, the servant of God in whom the nation's God-guided history is recapitulated and brought to completion, and also as the seed of Abraham in whom all the nations of the earth find blessing. Through his atoning death, which did away with the typical sacrificial services for ever, believing Jews and Gentiles become in him the people of God on earth. Baptism, the New Testament initiatory sign corresponding to circumcision, represents primarily union with Christ in his death and resurrection – the sole way of entry into the church.

Thus, the New Testament church has Abraham as its father, Jerusalem as its mother and place of worship, and the Old Testament as its Bible.

The New Testament idea of the church is reached by superimposing upon the notion of the covenant people of God the further thought that the church is the company of those who share in the redemptive renewal of a sin-spoiled creation which began when Jesus rose from the dead. As the individual believer is a new creation in Christ, raised with him out of death into life, possessed and led by the life-giving Holy Spirit, so also is the church as a whole.[1]

Just as God works to make a perfect whole out of his church, so he is at work in the life of every individual Christian.

Imagine a site occupied by a functioning business. The buildings in which the firm works are being pulled down, one by one, and new and better buildings are being put up in their place, using materials that originally belonged to what was demolished. While this goes on, business continues as usual, except for various temporary arrangements which call for patience. The constant changes are wearisome to those who have to keep the business going and who are not always told in advance about each successive disruption.

But in fact the architect has a master-plan for all stages of the rebuilding and a most competent manager directs and oversees every step. On a day-to-day basis there always proves to be a way of keeping the business going. Thus each day those involved in the business can truly feel that they have fulfilled their responsibility to serve the public, even though it wasn't as perfect as they would have wanted it to be.

The site and the business that goes on there represent our lives. God is constantly at work on the site, demolishing our bad habits and forming Christlike habits in their places. The Father has a master-plan for this progressive operation. Christ, through the Spirit, is executing this plan on a day-to-day basis. Though it involves frequent disruptions of routine and periodic bewilderments as to what God is up to, the overall effect of the work continues to increase our capacity for serving God and others.[2]

Reflection

Are you aware of being under construction or reconstruction? It might be good to consider and give thanks for progress so far.

Is progress painful? If so, C. S. Lewis' suggestion – that God is wanting to make of us not just an ordinary building but a palace fit for him to live in – could be some consolation. Meanwhile it's work in progress and fair enough to tell our self-critical hearts or our judgmental 'friends': 'Be patient – God 'aint finished with me yet!'

Taught by the Spirit

11

Reality in focus

Reading: 2 Timothy 3:14–16

... continue in what you have learned and have become convinced of, because you know those from whom you learned it, and how from infancy you have known the holy Scriptures, which are able to make you wise for salvation through faith in Christ Jesus. All Scripture is God-breathed and is useful for teaching, rebuking, correcting and training in righteousness, so that the man of God may be thoroughly equipped for every good work.

If while looking at you I should take my glasses off, I should reduce you to a smudge. I should still know you were there; I might still be able to tell whether you were male or female; I could probably manage to avoid bumping into you. But you would have become so indistinct at the edges and your features would be so blurred that adequate description of you, save from memory, would be quite beyond me. Should a stranger enter the room while my glasses were off, I could point to him, no doubt, but his face would be a blob and I would never know the expression on it. You and he would be right out of focus, so far as I was concerned, until I was bespectacled again.

One of Calvin's rare illustrations compares the way purblind persons like me need glasses to put print and people in focus with the way we all need Scripture to bring into focus our genuine sense of the divine. Though Calvin stated this comparison in general terms only, he clearly had in mind specific biblical truths as the lens whereby clear focus is achieved. Everyone, Calvin thought, has inklings of the reality of God, but they are vague and smudged. Getting God in focus means thinking correctly about his character, his sovereignty, his salvation, his love, his Son, his Spirit, and all the realities of his work and ways; it also means thinking rightly about our relationship to him as creatures either under sin or under grace, either living the responsive life of faith, hope, and love or living unresponsively in barrenness and gloom of heart. How can we learn to think correctly about these things? By learning of them from Scripture.[1]

Imagine a seminar in which the instructor, himself an authority, comments on someone else's essay so skilfully and profoundly that you, as a member of his class, learn all you need to know about the subject just by listening. This is how God teaches us from the Bible through the Holy Spirit. We are drawn into the middle of God's dealings with Bible characters and his address in and through the biblical books to their original recipients. By observing and overhearing, we learn what God thought of their attitudes, assumptions, ambitions, and activities, and what changes in their mindset and lifestyle he wanted to see, and this shows us what he must think of us and what changes he must want to see in us.

Now imagine yourself being coached at tennis. If the coach knows his stuff, you are likely to experience him as a perfect pest. You make strokes as you have done for years, the natural, comfortable way. He interrupts,

'Hey, not like that; that's no good; do it this way instead.' In the same way God corrects us, constantly working to change us.

Understanding, in a biblical sense, is a matter of receiving that *teaching* (first illustration) and *reproof* and *correction* that leads to *training in righteousness* (second illustration) for which Paul said Scripture was *profitable*. It means knowing what God's truth requires today in our lives.[2]

Reflection

Write down specific examples of how the Bible (read, expounded, explained, demonstrated in someone's life) has taught, trained, rebuked or corrected you and/or is teaching, training, rebuking or correcting you:

What difference has this made (is this making) to your life and work?

12

Inspired truth

Reading: 2 Peter 1:16–21

We did not follow cleverly invented stories when we told you about the power and coming of our Lord Jesus Christ, but we were eye-witnesses of his majesty. For he received honour and glory from God the Father when the voice came to him from the Majestic Glory, saying, 'This is my Son, whom I love; with him I am well pleased.' We ourselves heard this voice that came from heaven when we were with him on the sacred mountain.

And we have the word of the prophets made more certain, and you will do well to pay attention to it, as to a light shining in a dark place, until the day dawns and the morning star rises in your hearts. Above all, you must understand that no prophecy of Scripture came about by the prophet's own interpretation. For prophecy never had its origin in the will of man, but men spoke from God as they were carried along by the Holy Spirit.

The word translated 'inspired by God' really means '*breathed out* by God', the product of his creative Spirit, as the world itself was. The Bible analysis of inspiration is that 'men spoke from God as they were carried along by the Holy Spirit' and the documents resulting from inspiration are both man's witness to God and God's witness to himself. What is said of the Lord Jesus must also be said of the biblical books: he was and they are both fully human and fully divine. This is how our Lord and the apostles could quote the Old Testament both as what Moses, David, and Isaiah said, for example, and also as what God or the Holy Spirit said.

It appears that sometimes the processes of inspiration were conscious and sometimes not. Certainly the inspired writers were not psychologically passive, writing at dictation; their individuality comes out clearly in all that they wrote. But this does not put question marks against their inspiration, any more than the genuineness of our Lord's manhood throws doubt on the truth of his deity.

Being God's own teaching, the Bible may properly be called a revelation. First and foremost, however, we should think of it as the inspired record and interpretation of the revelation which God gave in history by visions and verbal messages, by mighty acts of mercy and judgment, and supremely by the life, death, and resurrection of the Lord Jesus Christ.[1]

Scripture is more sure than any other source of knowledge, just because it is directly and essentially the testimony, word, or witness of God. 'I have put my words in your mouth' (Jer. 1:9) – this was not only a promise to Jeremiah but also an explanation of divine inspiration. And in the New Testament it is acknowledged that God put his words into the mouths of, for instance, David and Isaiah.

This view of Scripture is not the instrumental view of inspiration which some hold: the view that Scripture is essentially human witness (albeit God-aided) to God and his grace, through which God somehow speaks to us a word that is not fully identical with what the Bible says. Peter and the others regarded Scripture rather as the human form of God's own witness. Just as in the person of Jesus we see the Son of God taking on human nature while his essential identity remains divine, so in the Scriptures we see the human form which God's word took while its essential identity as God's Word remained constant.

Men, borne along by the Holy Spirit, spoke from God. Their word is the Word of God because it is divine in origin. And because the Bible is the Word (communication, instruction, message) of God, it is utterly trustworthy and utterly authoritative for our lives – not just relatively so, as being the best source that we have, but absolutely so, as being God's pure word of address which stands for all eternity.[2]

Reflection

How do you approach Bible reading? Be honest as you complete the following:
 I approach Bible reading/read the Bible
 out of habit
 from a sense of duty
 expecting to hear from God
 with a willingness to learn, change, grow

INSPIRED TRUTH

Write a prayer, asking the Holy Spirit to inspire you as you read the words he inspired. If Bible reading has lost its sparkle for you, ask the Spirit of truth to light up God's truth again for you.

13

The unity of Scripture

Reading: 1 Peter 1:10–12

Concerning this salvation, the prophets, who spoke of the grace that was to come to you, searched intently and with the greatest care, trying to find out the time and circumstances to which the Spirit of Christ in them was pointing when he predicted the sufferings of Christ and the glories that would follow. It was revealed to them that they were not serving themselves but you, when they spoke of the things that have now been told you by those who have preached the gospel to you by the Holy Spirit sent from heaven. Even angels long to look into these things.

Because the Bible is a human book and God chose to convey his teaching to us in the form of the inspired instruction of his human penmen, the way into his mind is necessarily via their minds. So the basic discipline in biblical interpretation must always be the attempt to determine as exactly as possible just what the writer meant by the words he wrote and how he would explain the sense of his statements could we cross-question him about them.

THE UNITY OF SCRIPTURE

Because the Bible is a divine book, its sixty-six separate documents being products of a single divine mind proclaiming a single message, we must seek to integrate the fruit of our study of the individual books and writers into a single coherent whole. We know that the human author's thoughts are God's own thoughts too. As we seek to synthesise all the different thoughts, we become aware that at point after point God's thoughts go further and embrace more than those of any human writer did or could. The full significance of each passage only appears when it is set in the context of all the rest of Scripture – which its own human author, of course, was never able to do.

The Bible appears like a symphony orchestra with the Holy Spirit as its Toscanini: each instrumentalist has been brought willingly, spontaneously, creatively, to play his notes just as the great conductor desired, in full harmony with each other, though none of them could ever hear the music as a whole. We, however, are privileged to do precisely that.[1]

It is very important that we approach Scripture as the Word of God, not just as a mixed bag of human reflections and testimonies, some of which are likely to be more right-minded and some less, so that our main job is to pick out which are which. This is very inhibiting to fruitful dealing with the Scriptures.

As I look around the churches I see a broad division between pastoral leaders whose attitude to the Bible is generally one of trust because they take the Bible as coming from God, and those whose attitude is fundamentally one of mistrust because they see it only as a very mixed collection of human testimonies. Some of these people have been stumbled by what they've learned in seminary – or, as speakers of British and Canadian English say, in theological college – because it has been fashionable for a long time in these institutions to highlight the human aspects of Scripture and spend time dwelling on the differences, real or fancied, between the viewpoint of one writer and another. The effect of this can be to leave students adrift in a sea of pluralistic relativism, with a bewildering sense that the Bible offers a lot of different points of view and who can say which is right?

I am not questioning the value of these studies of the human side of Scripture but I see a need to balance them in a way that not all institutions do. I would balance them by saying to all Bible students, 'Remember, all Scripture proceeds from a single source, a single mind, the mind of God the Holy Spirit, and you have not taken its measure until you can see its divine unity underlying its human variety.'[2]

Reflection

Can you slot in some time in the coming months to think about the Bible as a whole and to skim-read whole chunks of it to get an overview of it?

Whether you can or not, spend a few moments now thinking about both the 'divine unity' and the 'human variety' evident in the Bible.

What are some of the strands and themes uniting all the books?

THE UNITY OF SCRIPTURE

Identify some aspects of human variety, in terms of different personalities, writers, styles of writing, in the Bible.

You might also like to consider how the divine unity/human variety principle works out in other areas, e.g. your church fellowship.

Lots of potential for further Bible study and discussion here!

14

Receptive to truth

Reading: 1 John 2:20–27

You have an anointing from the Holy One, and all of you know the truth. I do not write to you because you do not know the truth, but because you do know it and because no lie comes from the truth. Who is the liar? It is the man who denies that Jesus is the Christ. Such a man is the antichrist – he denies the Father and the Son. No one who denies the Son has the Father; whoever acknowledges the Son has the Father also.

See that what you have heard from the beginning remains in you. If it does, you also will remain in the Son and in the Father. And this is what he promised us – even eternal life.

I am writing these things to you about those who are trying to lead you astray. As for you, the anointing you received from him remains in you, and you do not need anyone to teach you. But as his anointing teaches you about all things and as that anointing is real, not counterfeit – just as it has taught you, remain in him.

RECEPTIVE TO TRUTH

It is the promised privilege of all Christians to be taught by God, and it is the Spirit of God who teaches them. The Spirit who taught all things to the apostles is the anointing that teaches all Christ's people – not by fresh disclosures of hitherto unknown truth, but by enabling us to recognise the divinity and bow to the authority of divine realities set before us.

But are we open to this working of the Spirit? As long as we approach the Scriptures with detachment, concerned only to appreciate them historically or aesthetically, and as long as we treat them merely as a human record, we scarcely are. We are only open to the Spirit's ministry to the degree we are willing to step inside the Bible and take our stand with the men to whom God spoke – Abraham listening to God in Ur, Moses listening to God at Sinai, the Israelites listening to God's Word from the lips of Moses and the prophets, the Jews listening to Jesus, the Romans and Corinthians and Timothy listening to Paul and so on – and to share joint tutorials with them, noting what God said to them and then seeking to see, in the light of that, what he would say to us.

Most of us are not that willing – we are prejudiced, lazy, and unprepared for the exercise of spirit and conscience that it involves. But greater willingness and increased receptiveness are themselves the Spirit's gifts. Therefore we must use the prayer, 'Teach me your decrees' (Ps. 119:12), as a plea not only for teaching but for teachableness.[1]

God gives understanding of the Bible through the Holy Spirit. That does not cancel out the need for study any more than it invalidates the rules of interpretation. Never oppose the work of the Spirit in giving understanding to your work as a student seeking it; the Spirit works through our diligence, not our laziness. Understanding what God's written Word means for me comes through seeing what it meant when it was first put on paper and applying that to ourselves.

It is in application specifically that we need divine help. Bible commentaries, Bible classes, Bible lectures and courses, plus the church's regular expository ministry can give us fair certainty as to what Scripture meant. We should make full use of them to that end. But only through the Spirit's illumination shall we be able to see how the teaching applies to us in our situation. So we should look not only to the commentators for exegesis but also to the Spirit for the application.

I'd like to suggest three questions which we could ask as we read the Bible. What does this passage tell me about *God*: his character, power, and purpose; his work, will, and ways in creation, providence and grace? What does this passage tell me about *people*: the human situation, man's possibilities, privileges, problems, right and wrong ways of living, man in sin, and man in grace? What is all this showing me and saying to me about *myself* and my own life? Lift your heart to God and ask for the Spirit's help as you work through these three questions in the divine presence, and you will certainly be given understanding.[2]

Reflection

How teachable are you? What, if anything, is hindering you from being more teachable than you are? Think about temperament, acquired attitudes and the events or people behind them. How could you deal with these so that in future they don't hinder you from being more fully open to being taught by the Spirit? Make notes if this would be helpful.

RECEPTIVE TO TRUTH

Write a prayer expressing your reservations and your willingness to become more open and teachable.

15

Praying in the Spirit

Reading: Romans 8:25–27

If we hope for what we do not yet have, we wait for it patiently.

In the same way, the Spirit helps us in our weakness. We do not know what we ought to pray for, but the Spirit himself intercedes for us with groans that words cannot express. And he who searches our hearts knows the mind of the Spirit, because the Spirit intercedes for the saints in accordance with God's will.

'Pray in the Holy Spirit' (Jude 20). What does this mean?

It means that we are not to pray in our own strength or with our own insight, but with the strength and insight that God supplies through his Spirit in our hearts. There are at least three thoughts implicit in this idea.

To pray in the Spirit is to pray as a child of God. It is the Spirit who prompts the attitude which treats, approaches, and cries to God as our Father in heaven.

To pray in the Spirit also means to pray with our eyes

PRAYING IN THE SPIRIT 67

on God. The Spirit has been given to open our eyes to see the good things that God has for us. 'No eye has seen, no ear has heard, no mind has conceived, what God has prepared for those who love him. But God has revealed it to us by his Spirit' (1 Cor. 2:9–10). The Spirit is the teacher of God's people: he opens the eyes of our understanding and keeps us looking to God, focusing on him and his resources of grace and power so that we are able to pray with confidence.

To pray in the Spirit means, too, relying on the Spirit's support. Sometimes we want to pray for something, but we find that we can't put our thoughts and desires into words: we end up tongue-tied before the Lord. At such times, the Spirit in us is praying for us, and God knows what is the mind of the Spirit, because the Spirit intercedes for the saints according to the will of God. 'If we ask anything according to his will, he hears us' (1 John 5:14). But when we don't know what specifically to ask for, and can only bring a name or need before God in general terms, he hears us too. This also is prayer in the Spirit. That's a tremendously encouraging truth.[1]

Changing the question slightly: what does prayer in the Spirit include? Four elements, at least.

First, it is a matter of seeking, claiming, and making use of access to God through Christ. Then the Christian adores and thanks God for her acceptance through Christ and for the knowledge that through Christ her prayers are heard. Third, she asks for the Spirit's help to see and do what brings glory to Christ, knowing that both the Spirit and Christ himself intercede for her as she struggles to pray for rightness in her own life. Finally, the Spirit leads the believer to concentrate on God and his glory in Christ with a sustained, single-minded simplicity of attention and intensity of desire that no one ever knows unless it is spiritually wrought.

Prayer in the Spirit is prayer from the heart, springing from awareness of God, self, others, needs, and Christ. Whether it comes forth verbalised, as in the prayers and praises recorded in Scripture, or unverbalised, as when the contemplative gazes God-ward in love or the charismatic slips into glossolalia, is immaterial. He or she whose heart seeks God through Christ prays in the Spirit.[2]

Reflection

Bring before God the people for whom you don't know how to pray – through lack of wisdom, feeling too involved or churned up, or whatever. Ask the Spirit to intercede for you on their behalf. Stay in an attitude of expectant, thankful, heartfelt though wordless prayer for as long as possible.

Effective through the Spirit

16

Not grieving but filled

Reading: Ephesians 5:8–20

Live as children of light (for the fruit of the light consists in all goodness, righteousness and truth) and find out what pleases the Lord. Have nothing to do with the fruitless deeds of darkness, but rather expose them. For it is shameful even to mention what the disobedient do in secret. But everything exposed by the light becomes visible . . . This is why it is said:

> *'Wake up, O sleeper,*
> *rise from the dead,*
> *and Christ will shine on you.'*

Be very careful how you live – not as unwise but as wise, making the most of every opportunity, because the days are evil. Therefore do not be foolish, but understand what the Lord's will is. Do not get drunk on wine, which leads to debauchery. Instead, be filled with the Spirit. Speak to one another with psalms, hymns and spiritual songs. Sing and make music in your heart to the Lord, always giving thanks to God the Father for everything, in the name of our Lord Jesus Christ.

If anyone does not have the Spirit of Christ, he does not belong to Christ and what he needs to do is not search for the Spirit but rather come to Christ in faith and repentance, whereupon the Spirit will be given to him.

The important question then is: Does the Holy Spirit have you? Does he have all of you or only some parts of you? Do you grieve him or are you led by him? Do you rely on him to enable you to respond to Christ when he prompts you? Do you reckon with the fact that 'your body is a temple of the Holy Spirit, who is in you, whom you have received from God' (1 Cor. 6:19)? Do you revere his work within you and co-operate with it or obstruct it by thoughtlessness and carelessness, indiscipline and self-indulgence?

The specific questions must be understood Christ-centredly; in reality they are all ways of asking whether Christ your Saviour is Lord of your life. But to ask them in relation to the Spirit is to give them a force and a concreteness that otherwise they might not have. In the world of projecting pictures onto screens, this would be called sharpening the focus.

The Spirit indwells in us in order to transform us and works constantly in our hearts and minds to bring us closer to Christ and keep us there. As God resident within us, he himself is close to any foul thinking or behaviour in which we allow ourselves to engage. This thought should weigh with us when temptation comes.[1]

'Do not grieve the Holy Spirit of God,' Paul says (Eph. 4:30), and this plea is a witness both to the Spirit's personhood and to the fact that divine holiness is his nature. As with the first and second person of the Godhead so with the third: some ways of behaving please him and others distress and offend him. In the second category come bitterness, wrath, anger, clamour, slander, malice, and stealing (Eph. 4:28, 31), and in fact any other transgressions of moral law. For Christians to fall into these sins directly thwarts his purpose and spoils his work of making us Christlike. Knowledge that our bodies are temples of the Spirit and that this 'gracious, willing guest' is hard at work in our hearts to sanctify us should induce reverent awe and quickly shame us out of all moral laxity.

To dissuade us against grieving the Spirit, the Bible calls us to the positive counterpart – to be filled with the Spirit. The words imply a constant obligation. 'Filled' conveys the thought of being wholly concerned with and wholly controlled by the realities which the Spirit makes known, and the ideal of life to which he points us. From what source should satisfaction be sought? Not from indulgence to alcohol (the worldly person's way of raising his enjoyment level), but from being occupied entirely with the Spirit's concerns. Then we shall have something to sing about, for the gratified Holy Spirit will sustain in us a joy which the worldly person never knows.[2]

Reflection

As an act of the will, symbolised in any way with which you feel comfortable, release to God and empty yourself of what grieves the Spirit as he looks into your heart and life. Then pray for the Spirit to fill you completely. If it helps, imagine the negative things flowing out and the Holy Spirit and all that he brings flooding in.

You may like to note down what you let go of or threw out.

Regularly, or even just occasionally, prefacing prayer times and Bible reading with a few moments of self-preparation like this, could lift them into a new dimension.

17

Ready for battle

Reading: Ephesians 6:10–17

... Be strong in the Lord and in his mighty power. Put on the full armour of God so that you can take your stand against the devil's schemes. For our struggle is not against flesh and blood, but against the rulers, against the authorities, against the powers of this dark world and against the spiritual forces of evil in the heavenly realms. Therefore put on the full armour of God, so that when the evil day comes, you may be able to stand your ground, and after you have done everything, to stand. Stand firm then, with the belt of truth buckled round your waist, with the breastplate of righteousness in place, and with your feet fitted with the readiness that comes from the gospel of peace. In addition to all this, take up the shield of faith, with which you can extinguish all the flaming arrows of the evil one. Take the helmet of salvation and the sword of the Spirit, which is the word of God.

The helmet protects the head against stunning, crushing blows. For the Christian soldier, God provides the helmet

LIFE IN THE SPIRIT

of salvation, which I believe means assurance of salvation, present and future. We can't be knocked out by Satan if we are sure that now, tomorrow, and for all eternity we are safe in the hands of God who holds us securely and will keep us for ever by his power.

The helmet, belt, breastplate, shoes, shield, are *defensive* weapons. Next Paul names an *offensive* weapon: 'the sword of the Spirit, which is the word of God'. We are to take this and use it as Jesus used it when he was tempted. Satan made suggestions and each time Jesus quoted Scripture and said in effect: 'It is by this word of my Father, not by any of your words, that I am going to live. So get away from me, Satan.' Thus he resisted the devil, using the sword of the Spirit, and the devil retreated. That is how we are to use the Word of God when Satan comes to tempt us: we are to set it like a brandished sword between him and ourselves.[1]

Right at the beginning of Jesus' ministry he was taken into the wilderness to be tempted by the devil, and we read of him showing Satan his resolve to do the will of God at all costs.

I may be wrong, but I think that the way the devil tempted Jesus was not by appearing and identifying himself ('this is your tempter speaking . . .'), but by injecting ideas into his mind. Jesus found himself beset by these strong ideas: 'Command this stone to become bread . . . Worship me (Satan) . . . Throw yourself down.' The moment Jesus asked himself where these ideas came from, he knew and rejected them.

The devil was saying to him in effect: 'This is how you could have the world as your kingdom. Give the people what they want – food, to start with. Play my game and appeal to the instincts which people under my rule recognise. Dazzle them with a show of personal invulnerability. Then they'll eat out of your hand!' But all that was the opposite of God's plan.

Jesus told Satan (it is often good sense to talk out loud to the devil) that neither he nor the people to whom he would minister were going to live on bread alone; they were going to live by the Word of God. He would not worship Satan or look to Satan for any gift because the Bible states that God alone is to be worshipped and trusted. Nor would he presumptuously put his heavenly Father to the test, which was what he would have done by throwing himself down from a pinnacle of the temple. Satan had misapplied Scripture in suggesting that God's promise of protection was an invitation to suicidal action.

Jesus is our example of mature discipleship in recognising the devil's temptations as they cut across God's Word, in rejecting the satanic suggestions, and in asserting that he would go God's way and live by Scripture, whatever happens. Like Jesus, we can throw the Book at Satan, or – to put it another way – wield the sword of the Spirit; while doing so, we should pray that Jesus himself will drive him back.[2]

Reflection

What do you understand by the images of weapons and armour and by the instruction to put them on or use them?

  belt of truth
  breastplate of righteousness
  feet ready with the gospel of peace
  shield of faith
  sword of the Spirit

Are you facing a particular temptation at this time? Can you imagine the words that the devil might use if he were tempting you as specifically and articulately as he tempted Jesus in Luke 4:1–12? Now, can you find a sword-thrust (Bible verse or biblical guideline) which effectively says 'No' to him, followed by a 'Yes' if he counter-attacks with 'Did God really say such and such?'

18

Prayer – how?

Readings: John 16:23–27; 1 John 5:13–15

In that day you will no longer ask me anything. I tell you the truth, my Father will give you whatever you ask in my name. Until now you have not asked for anything in my name. Ask and you will receive, and your joy will be complete.

Though I have been speaking figuratively, a time is coming when I will no longer use this kind of language but will tell you plainly about my Father. In that day you will ask in my name. I am not saying that I will ask the Father on your behalf. No, the Father himself loves you because you have loved me and have believed that I came from God.

I write these things to you who believe in the name of the Son of God so that you may know that you have eternal life. This is the confidence that we have in approaching God: that if we ask anything according to his will, he hears us. And if we know that he hears us – whatever we ask – we know that we have what we asked of him.

80 LIFE IN THE SPIRIT □

Meditation – thinking about God in God's presence – is a helpful preparation for speaking to God directly and one which we seem to need regularly. In this world, interviews with persons of some standing are handled with ceremony, both out of respect for the persons themselves and also in order to gain most benefit from the interview.

To rush to God randomly babbling about what is on our mind at the moment, with no pause to realise his greatness and grace and our own sinfulness and smallness, is at once to dishonour him and to make shallow our own fellowship with him. I, for one, want to do better than that. Like others, I find it good to preface my prayers about needs by reading Scripture and thinking through what my reading shows me of God and turning that vision into praise before I go further.

A little reverent thought about God before opening our mouths to address him makes a lot of difference in the quality of fellowship with him that follows. Remembering, and reviewing who God is, is never time wasted; it is, rather, a vital means of *knowing* God, just as prayer itself is.[1]

Read again our two passages which seek to lead us deeper into prayer than most of us have ever gone.

The aim of prayer is not to force God's hand or make him do our will against his own, but to deepen our knowledge of him and our fellowship with him through contemplating his glory, confessing our dependence and need, and consciously embracing his goals. Our asking therefore must be *according to God's will* and *in Jesus' name*.

The context of such asking is assured faith. In that day when Jesus teaches them, by the Spirit, plainly of the Father, there will be no question of enlisting Jesus' support in prayer, as if he were more merciful than the Father or could influence him in a way that they could not; in that day they will know inwardly that as believers they are the Father's beloved.

To ask in Jesus' name is not to use a verbal spell but

to base our asking on Christ's saving relationship to us through the Cross; this will involve making petitions which Christ can endorse and put his name to. When God answers in Jesus' name, he gives *through* Jesus as our mediator and *to* Jesus as the one who will be glorified through what is given.

Central to the life of prayer is letting ourselves be taught by Christ through his Word and Spirit what we should pray for. To the extent that we *know*, through the Spirit's inner witness, that we are making a request which the Lord has specifically given us to make, to that extent we *know* that we have the answer even before we see it.[2]

Reflection

Meditate on the name of Jesus. What verses, events, images, pictures, memories, feelings . . . does it conjure up? Make notes if you wish.

Soak in all that richness. Perhaps it will inspire you to write a song or poem on what the name of Jesus means to you . . .

19

Prayer – for what?

Reading: Colossians 1:3–14

We always thank God, the Father of our Lord Jesus Christ, when we pray for you, because we have heard of your faith in Christ Jesus and of the love you have for all the saints – the faith and love that spring from the hope that is stored up for you in heaven and that you have already heard about in the word of truth, the gospel that has come to you. All over the world this gospel is bearing fruit and growing, just as it has been doing among you since the day you heard it and understood God's grace in all its truth. You learned it from Epaphras, our dear fellow-servant, who is a faithful minister of Christ on our behalf, and who also told us of your love in the Spirit.

For this reason, since the day we heard about you, we have not stopped praying for you and asking God to fill you with the knowledge of his will through all spiritual wisdom and understanding. And we pray this in order that you may live a life worthy of the Lord and may please him in every way: bearing fruit in every good work, growing in the knowledge of God, being strengthened with all power according to his glorious might so that you may have great endurance and patience, and joyfully giving thanks to the Father, who has qualified you to share in the inheritance of the saints in the kingdom of light. For he has rescued us from the dominion of darkness and brought us into the kingdom of the Son he loves, in whom we have redemption, the forgiveness of sins.

Each Christian's prayer life, like every good marriage, has in it common factors about which one can generalise and also uniquenesses which no other Christian's prayer life will quite match. You are you, and I am I, and we must each find our own way to God; and there is no recipe for prayer that can work for us like a handyman's do-it-yourself manual or a cookery book, where the claim is that if you follow the instructions you can't go wrong.

Praying is not like carpentry or cookery; it is the active exercise of a personal relationship: a kind of friendship with the living God and his Son Jesus Christ, and the way it goes is more under divine control than under ours. Books on praying, like marriage manuals, are not to be treated with slavish superstition, as if the perfection of technique is the answer to all difficulties; their purpose, rather, is to suggest things to try. But as in other close relationships, in prayer you have to find out by trial and error what is right for you, and you learn to pray by praying.

Some of us talk more, others less; some are constantly vocal, others cultivate silence before God as their way of adoration; some slip into glossolalia, others make a point of not slipping into it; yet we may all be praying as God means us to do. The only rule is: Stay within the biblical guidelines, and within those guidelines, as John Chapman put it, 'Pray as you can, and don't try to pray as you can't.'[1]

Praying for fellow Christians is a basic Christian responsibility. Our passage helps us to see how to discharge it. Paul asks God to give the Colossian Christians four things:

Christian knowledge: He prays that they will know both God's will (his plans, ways, and commands) and God himself. The Greek word for knowledge implies full, thorough knowledge, as does the verb 'filled'. 'Understanding' relates to principles of truth, 'wisdom' to application of those principles in life. Worthy living depends on this knowledge; he who does not know God's will cannot do it. Knowledge of God increases as we live up to it.

Christian practice: He prays that they will lead a life worthy of Christ the king to whom they owe their salvation, and a life pleasing to God at every point by every activity.

Christian patience: He prays for their cheerful endurance in dealing with trying people and situations with actual rejoicing as tribulation grinds on. Paul specifies that all God's strength, power, and might are needed to produce such a reaction!

Christian thankfulness: He prays that they will be grateful for grace, the major motive of Christian living. According to the truth of the gospel, Christian doctrine is grace throughout and Christian ethics are gratitude all the way.[2]

Reflection

Is there a person or group whom you promised to pray for but have rather neglected in your intercessions? How about writing a prayer for that person or group now, based on what Paul prayed for the Colossian church, and praying it regularly in the coming days, weeks or months?

20

Prayer – for whom?

Ephesians 6:18–19

Pray in the Spirit on all occasions with all kinds of prayers and requests. With this in mind, be alert and always keep on praying for all the saints.

Pray also for me, that whenever I open my mouth, words may be given me so that I will fearlessly make known the mystery of the gospel, for which I am an ambassador in chains. Pray that I may declare it fearlessly, as I should.

Here we have a little directory of prayer. Notice the four 'alls': 'at all times', 'with all prayer', 'with all perseverance', and 'for all the saints' in the RSV of the passage.

These verses have something to say about the nature, the time, the enabler, the discipline, the matter, and the range of prayer. All these deserve study but I want to focus now on the range of prayer suggested.

We're not to pray just for ourselves but for all the saints, all the family of God – or at least for all the family members known to us and involved with us in some way.

We need to ask God which of his saints and which of their activities in particular he wants us to be praying for on a regular basis. Let the Lord lead here. He leads Christians differently in these matters.

Some feel they should pray intensively for a small range of people and concerns; others less intensively for a wider range. However, the general formula, whichever way he leads you in detail, is that we are to make supplication for all the saints as they and their needs are known to us. Christian prayer must be family-oriented, not just individual-oriented. There's to be a network of mutual service not only at the level of face-to-face contact and personal helpfulness, but also at the level of intercession for one another at God's throne of grace. Christian fellowship must include this discipline of praying for one another.[1]

We should seek from God the requests to make in each situation and recognise that it is the Holy Spirit's task, in addition to the rest of his ministry in our prayers, to guide us here as we lay the facts before the Lord. Often we enjoy no special leading and are only enabled to pray for needs in general terms, but sometimes the Spirit prompts very specific requests and leads us to make them with unusual confidence.

Once the theological institution of which I was principal was going to be closed by episcopal order. The community fixed a day of prayer about it. Two hours into the day, I found I knew exactly what to ask God for: a merger with another institution on specific terms so controversial that they seemed unrealistic. I could share this with no one at the time, but I held to the vision as best I could, and within a year all I had been led to pray for happened. Glory to God!

Again, a friend was in the hospital for an exploratory operation; cancer symptoms were present. Many prayed. Laying the situation before God, I found myself drawn (for the only time in my life so far) to pray specifically and confidently for a miracle of healing. Walking home from church on Sunday morning and praying thus, I felt I was being told that the prayer was heard and I need not continue to press it. On Monday the operation revealed no trace of cancer. Once more, glory to God!

We must always be consciously open to being led by God in the things we pray for.[2]

Reflection

Before praying for others today, with the Spirit's help, spend time listening to God for the requests that would really be in line with their needs and with his glory and will.

If you need help with inner stillness and receptivity, look around for what's available in terms of books and courses on listening.

One in the Spirit

21

Wholehearted worship

Reading: Romans 11:33–12:2

*Oh, the depths of the riches of the
  wisdom and knowledge of God!
How unsearchable his judgments,
  and his paths beyond tracing out!
'Who has known the mind of the Lord?
  Or who has been his counsellor?'
'Who has ever given to God,
  that God should repay him?'
For from him and through him
  and to him are all things.
To him be the glory for ever! Amen.*

Therefore, I urge you, brothers, in view of God's mercy, to offer your bodies as living sacrifices, holy and pleasing to God – this is your spiritual act of worship. Do not conform any longer to the pattern of this world, but be transformed by the renewing of your mind. Then you will be able to test and approve what God's will is – his good, pleasing and perfect will.

The central issue of belief today is between faith in one God (monotheism) and disbelief in any God (atheism); but in Bible times it was between believing in one God and in many (polytheism). The Bible is hot against polytheism, for one who believes in many gods cannot regard any of them as having absolute power or total claim on his life, nor dare he serve any of them exclusively to the disregard of others. But Scripture insists throughout that there is only one God, the Maker and Lord of all.

So what is this one God like? To the fourth question of the Westminster Shorter Catechism, 'What is God?' the following answer is returned: 'God is a Spirit, infinite, eternal, and unchangeable in his being, wisdom, power, holiness, justice, goodness, and truth.' No better account of God has ever been framed in so few words. Two points stand out:

First, *God's existence is eternal*. He is God 'from everlasting to everlasting', all-powerful, all-knowing, self-sustaining, and needing nothing.

Second, *God's character is unchanging*. This is how he proclaimed himself to Moses: 'The LORD, the LORD, the compassionate and gracious God, slow to anger, abounding in love and faithfulness, maintaining love to thousands, and forgiving wickedness, rebellion and sin. Yet he does not leave the guilty unpunished' (Exod. 34:6–7). This is God's character still, for he cannot deny himself.[1]

To worship God is to recognise his worth or worthiness; to look God-ward, and to acknowledge in all appropriate ways the value of what we see. The Bible calls this activity 'glorifying God' or 'giving glory to God', and views it as the ultimate end, and from one point of view, the whole duty of man.

Scripture views the glorifying of God as a sixfold activity: praising God for all that he is and all his achievements; thanking him for his gifts and his goodness to us; asking him to meet our own and others' needs; offering him our gifts, our service, and ourselves; learning of him from his Word, read and preached, and obeying his voice;

telling others of his worth, both by public confession and testimony to what he has done for us. Thus we might say that the basic formulas of worship are these: 'Lord, you are wonderful'; 'Thank you, Lord'; 'Please, Lord'; 'Take this, Lord'; 'Yes, Lord'; 'Listen everybody!'

This then is worship in its largest sense: petition as well as praise, preaching as well as prayer, hearing as well as speaking, actions as well as words, obeying as well as offering, loving people as well as loving God. However, the primary acts of worship are those which focus on God directly – and we must not imagine that work for God in the world is a substitute for direct fellowship with him in praise and prayer and devotion.[2]

Reflection

Meditate on the following:
Worship is the submission of all our nature to God. It is the quickening of conscience by his holiness; the nourishment of mind with his truth; the purifying of imagination by his beauty; the opening of the heart to his love; the surrender of the will to his purpose – and all this gathered up in adoration, the most selfless emotion of which our nature is capable and therefore the chief remedy for that self-centredness which is our original sin and the source of all actual sin.[3]

Respond as you can and feel able to – through prayer, through an act symbolising your inner attitude, through a decision about your future priorities . . .

22

Healthy unity

Reading: Ephesians 4:3–7, 11–16

Make every effort to keep the unity of the Spirit through the bond of peace. There is one body and one Spirit – just as you were called to one hope when you were called – one Lord, one faith, one baptism; one God and Father of all, who is over all and through all and in all.

But to each one of us grace has been given as Christ apportioned it . . . It was he who gave some to be apostles, some to be prophets, some to be evangelists, and some to be pastors and teachers, to prepare God's people for works of service, so that the body of Christ may be built up until we all reach unity in the faith and in the knowledge of the Son of God and become mature, attaining to the whole measure of the fullness of Christ.

Then we will no longer be infants, tossed back and forth by the waves, and blown here and there by every wind of teaching and by the cunning and craftiness of men in their deceitful scheming. Instead, speaking the truth in love, we will in all things grow up into him who is the Head, that is, Christ. From him the whole body, joined and held together by every supporting ligament, grows and builds itself up in love, as each part does its work.

The body was Paul's standard illustration for making clear the inner life of the church. There is one church universal which is invisible in its own nature. It is the company of those who have living faith in Christ and so are united to each other because they are united to him. But that church becomes visible wherever the people of God, either many or few, meet together to worship, pray, maintain the ministry of the Word, spread the gospel, have fellowship, celebrate the sacraments, and share the things of God. So Paul writing to the local church at Corinth says, 'You are the body of Christ' (1 Cor. 12:27).

He would say the same thing, no doubt, to every congregation he was privileged to address. For each local congregation is a small-scale presentation and an authentic sample of the church universal. Therefore, when people look at any congregation, they should see the life of the world church concentrated in that one place.

What sort of life should it be? Body life, the life in which all limbs are contributing to the welfare of the whole body. Our bodies give us trouble when any part is not working properly, but when the parts work properly, the body's life is a wonderful thing. In the same way Paul wants us to understand that the life of a church is a wonderful thing as, in the power of God's Spirit, each limb, unit, bit, piece, joint, and muscle does its best and contributes to the health of the whole.[1]

Body life is a term for the network of mutual relationships which Christ both calls and causes the limbs of his body to build. Scripture spells out the ethics of body life in terms of valuation and service.

The racial, social, economic, cultural, and sexual

distinctions which operate as restraints on our acceptance and appreciation of each other cannot be abolished. However, the limits they impose must be transcended. In Christ's body all must welcome and value each other as 'members one of another'. You might not think it from watching what goes on in our churches, but God wants life in his new society to be a perfect riot of affection, goodwill, openheartedness, and friendship. So what on earth are we all playing at? You tell me!

Service is love in action. Christ's body 'builds itself up in love'. This love is more than sweet talk or sweet smiles; its measure is the evil that you avoid inflicting and the good you go out of your way to do. How is the church upbuilt or edified in love? By each part working properly in fellowship: sharing what by God's gift we have and are. This sharing is the service or ministry to which every Christian is called. Either we all advance towards Christlike maturity together through mutual ministry (lay people to lay people and also to clergy and vice versa), or we all stagnate separately.[2]

Reflection

Identify any 'them and us' attitudes which could make it harder for your fellowship to be 'a perfect riot of affection, goodwill, openheartedness, and friendship'. How do attitudes change? How could your attitudes start to change?

23

Genuine fellowship

Reading: Galatians 5:25–6:6

Since we live by the Spirit, let us keep in step with the Spirit. Let us not become conceited, provoking and envying each other.

Brothers, if someone is caught in a sin, you who are spiritual should restore him gently. But watch yourself, or you also may be tempted. Carry each other's burdens, and in this way you will fulfil the law of Christ. If anyone thinks he is something when he is nothing, he deceives himself. Each one should test his own actions. Then he can take pride in himself, without comparing himself to somebody else, for each one should carry his own load.

Anyone who receives instructions in the word must share all good things with his instructor.

Christian fellowship is an expression of both love and humility; it springs from the wish to help and the wish to be helped; it is a corporate seeking by Christian people to know God better through sharing with each other what individually they have learned already. And here are three further truths about fellowship.

First, it is *a means of grace*. Through and in fellowship, our souls are refreshed and fed by the effort to communicate our knowledge of divine things, to help and pray for others, and to receive from God through them.

Second, fellowship is *a test of life*. Fellowship means opening our hearts to our fellow Christians. The person who discards pretence when talking with his fellow believers is the one who is being open and honest in his daily dealings with God. He is the one who is walking in the light.

Third, fellowship is *a gift of God*. 'May the grace of the Lord Jesus Christ and the love of God and *the fellowship of the Holy Spirit* be with you all' (2 Cor. 13:14). It is only where the Holy Spirit has been given, where we are spiritually alive to God and anxious to grow in grace ourselves and help others do the same, that true fellowship will be a possibility. It is only as the Spirit enables us that we shall actually be able to practise it.

Such fellowship can happen in preaching; as we pray together; in group Bible study; in talk between friends over a meal; in talk between husband and wife at home in the evening. But in every case, the Lord's presence and power will be realised through the words, attitudes, actions, and love of a fellow Christian.[1]

In Galatians chapter 5 Paul tells us to walk in the Spirit and serve one another in love, and in our reading he explains what that will mean. The law of Christ, he says, is precisely this: to bear others' burdens, accepting involvement in their troubles and laying ourselves out to help, support, and restore. It pleases God more that I should carry someone else's burden and let him carry mine than that we should each carry our own. The latter is the way of lonely isolation, one aspect of the fallen human condition; the former is the way of Christian fellowship.

Fellowship means sharing burdens as well as benefits:

we carry each other's luggage, both material and spiritual, and find relief and strength in doing so. This path of exchange – problem-sharing and burden-bearing – is Christ's image in our lives for it reflects his loving substitution for us under judgment on the cross. Paul summons his readers to burden-bearing as brothers in Christ and as spiritual men.

With the call to burden-bearing goes a warning against complacent conceit. Psychologically this is shrewd: those who seek to do good especially in counselling and rescue work are always tempted to feel they are a cut above those they are helping. Gentleness is called for here, since 'there but for the grace of God go I'.

The 'load' which 'each one should carry' has nothing to do with burden-bearing; it's his responsibility for his own life for which he must answer to God and reap what he has sown. Each of us, then, will be wise to test our own work and not rest in the thought that some are a lot worse than we are! Verse 6, so comforting to preachers, is not as isolated from Paul's theme as it looks. How else when pastors are impoverished (and they often are) should the rule of burden-bearing be applied?[2]

Reflection

Give thanks for the good things (you can use the criteria above) that are already happening in your church or other fellowship.

Only after doing that, identify one or two areas for improvement. Would setting an example yourself be

100   *LIFE IN THE SPIRIT*   □

more productive than telling others what they ought to be doing? And if you do need to say something, how about a lighthearted, humorous approach rather than coming on all heavy and judgmental?

24

Spiritual gifts

Reading: Romans 12:6–17,21

We have different gifts, according to the grace given us. If a man's gift is prophesying, let him use it in proportion to his faith. If it is serving, let him serve; if it is teaching, let him teach; if it is encouraging, let him encourage; if it is contributing to the needs of others, let him give generously; if it is leadership, let him govern diligently; if it is showing mercy, let him do it cheerfully.

Love must be sincere. Hate what is evil; cling to what is good. Be devoted to one another in brotherly love. Honour one another above yourselves. Never be lacking in zeal, but keep your spiritual fervour, serving the Lord. Be joyful in hope, patient in affliction, faithful in prayer. Share with God's people who are in need. Practise hospitality.

Bless those who persecute you; bless and do not curse. Rejoice with those who rejoice; mourn with those who mourn. Live in harmony with one another. Do not be proud, but be willing to be associated with people of low position. Do not be conceited.

Do not repay anyone evil for evil. Be careful to do what is right in the eyes of everybody . . .

Do not be overcome by evil, but overcome evil with good.

Fellowship, which means the give-and-take of sharing the things of God, is carried on through the reality of spiritual gifts. So what is a spiritual gift? It is in essence a God-given capacity to express or minister Christ so that those to whom the service is rendered will see Christ and grow in Christ, to his glory. It may be a gift of speech, behaviour, conduct, or service in any form. It may be the practical gift of relieving needs, Samaritan-style, or the teacher's gift of explaining things from God's Word. It may be a natural talent sanctified or an ability newly bestowed. But whatever form it takes, it is a God-given ability to make Christ known.

When gifts are exercised in the power of the Spirit by whom they are bestowed, the reality of the situation is this: Christ himself, on his throne but through his Spirit in us, is ministering still as he ministered to people in the days of his flesh. We become his mouth, his hands, his feet, to fulfil his ministry to others by exercising the spiritual gifts we have been given. Christ now ministers to his people through his people, and through them to other people too.

Usually others see our gifts better than we see them ourselves. Usually others can tell us more exactly what we can and cannot do for the Lord than we are able to discern by self-review and introspection. Realising then that the finding and use of gifts are fellowship business, we should ask others to watch us and tell us what our gifts are, and so be guided by them as we seek to serve.[1]

There are many gifts, and there is no reason to treat even 1 Corinthians 12:28–30 as an exhaustive list; indeed, it is doubtful in principle whether such a list could be compiled. Gifts vary in value according to whether they give more or less help to others; thus speaking the Word of God in intelligible terms is better than speaking in a tongue. What are the higher gifts? Those that communicate Christ best to others, showing them his reality either by word or by deed. Nor should gifts of service be rated below gifts of speech: each gift is equally important in its place.

Paul's charge to his readers to use their gifts starts with the ministry of the Word but soon broadens into a general plea for mutual service in the exercise of Christian graces towards others. No doubt gifts and graces are distinct in idea, but in practice much using of our gifts is a matter of exercising our graces informally and spontaneously in giving what help we can according to people's needs.

All can serve others in some way and all are called to do so; such service, whatever its form, falls under the definition of an exercise of gifts. And the purpose of all gifts is edification – building up Christians and leading them forward towards their ultimate perfection.[2]

Reflection

Spiritual gifts edify. That means they are good and do good. Reflect on what makes the difference between gifts that are good and do good and those that do more harm than good. Think about, for example: the needs and wishes of the recipient; the attitude of the giver to the recipient, reflected in his choice of gift and the manner in which it is given. How can our giving and use of gifts reflect more of God's nature and attitudes?

104   *LIFE IN THE SPIRIT*   □

For further study

Either or both of the following:

What is being taught and practised in your church in relation to spiritual gifts? How does it reflect or differ from the principles given in Romans 12 and 1 Corinthians 12 and the comments above on these passages?

What God-given abilities do you have for making Christ known – through the way you live and relate as well as through your words? Have you ever thought of these as your spiritual gifts? Are you putting them to good use in your home, church, workplace, neighbourhood?

25

Spiritual graces

Reading: John 13:3–17

Jesus knew that the Father had put all things under his power, and that he had come from God and was returning to God; so he got up from the meal, took off his outer clothing, and wrapped a towel round his waist. After that, he poured water into a basin and began to wash his disciples' feet, drying them with the towel that was wrapped round him.

He came to Simon Peter, who said to him, 'Lord, are you going to wash my feet?'

Jesus replied, 'You do not realise now what I am doing, but later you will understand.'

'No,' said Peter, 'you shall never wash my feet.'

Jesus answered, 'Unless I wash you, you have no part with me.'

'Then, Lord,' Simon Peter replied, 'not just my feet but my hands and head as well!'

Jesus answered, 'A person who has had a bath needs only to wash his feet; his whole body is clean. And you are clean, though not every one of you.' For he knew who was going to betray him, and that was why he said not every one was clean.

When he had finished washing their feet, he put on his clothes and returned to his place. 'Do you understand what I have done for you?' he asked them. 'You call me "Teacher" and "Lord", and rightly so, for that is what I am. Now that I, your Lord and Teacher, have washed your feet, you also should wash one another's feet. I have set you an example that you should do as I have done for you. I tell you the truth, no servant is greater than his master, nor is a messenger greater than the one who sent him. Now that you know these things, you will be blessed if you do them.'

What the Corinthians had to realise, and what some today may need to relearn, is that, as the Puritan John Owen put it, there can be *gifts* without *graces*; that is, we may be capable of performances that benefit others spiritually and yet be strangers ourselves to the Spirit-wrought inner transformation that true knowledge of God brings. The manifestation of the Spirit in charismatic performance is not the same thing as the fruit of the Spirit in Christlike character, and there may be much of the former with little or none of the latter. You can have many gifts and few graces; you can even have genuine gifts and no genuine graces at all, as did Balaam, Saul, and Judas. So no one should treat his gifts as proof that he pleases God or as guaranteeing his salvation. Spiritual gifts do neither of these things.

All through the New Testament, when God's work in human lives is spoken of, the ethical has priority over the charismatic. Christlikeness (not in gifts, but in love, humility, submission to the providence of God, and sensitiveness to the claims of people) is seen as what really matters.

Any mindset which treats the Spirit's gifts as more

important than his fruit is spiritually wrong-headed and needs correcting. The best corrective will be a view of the Spirit's work that sets activities and performances in a framework that displays them as acts of serving and honouring God and gives them value as such.[1]

In our reading, Jesus set us an unforgettable example. As the Son of God he knew he would soon return to his Father to reign: as searcher of hearts he knew which of his chosen disciples were 'clean' (i.e., forgiven and accepted by God) and which one was not 'clean' and would betray him. Also he knew that the road back to the Father led through the ultimate humiliation of the cross, the humiliation which he symbolised here by taking the role of a low-grade menial.

Jesus loved his own 'to the end' – not only to the end of his earthly life and of his redeeming work, but also to the nth degree. A Jewish host normally had his guests' feet washed by an underling; Jesus, as host of the supper, did the job himself, first taking off his coat to reveal himself as a true servant in action. A modern equivalent of feet-washing would be shoe-shining. And the particular blessing which this task signified was daily cleansing within an already established relationship of acceptance.

As teacher, lord, and director of his disciples' lives, Jesus charged them to follow his example of loving service. The particular service which the feet-washing signified was unique (i.e., cleansing from sin) but the spirit of love and care which the action revealed was not to be unique: Christians must reproduce it. Rather than displaying particular outward behaviour-patterns, Christians are called upon to imitate Christ by maintaining an attitude of self-humbling love.[2]

Reflection

Enter imaginatively into the incident described in the passage. 'Be' one of the disciples whose feet Jesus washes. What are your feelings? What effect and impact will Jesus' action and attitude have on you now and from now on? Make notes if you wish.

'. . . the ethical has priority over the charismatic.' Do you agree? Is this reflected in your life and the life of your church?

Experiencing the Spirit

26

Focus on Jesus

Reading: John 14:23–27

'If anyone loves me, he will obey my teaching. My Father will love him, and we will come to him and make our home with him. He who does not love me will not obey my teaching. These words you hear are not my own; they belong to the Father who sent me.

All this I have spoken while still with you. But the Counsellor, the Holy Spirit, whom the Father will send in my name, will teach you all things and will remind you of everything I have said to you. Peace I leave with you; my peace I give you. I do not give to you as the world gives. Do not let your hearts be troubled and do not be afraid.'

The Holy Spirit's distinctive role is to fulfil what we may call a floodlight ministry in relation to the Lord Jesus Christ. So far as this role was concerned, the Spirit had not been given while Jesus was on earth; only when the Father had glorified him could the Spirit's work of making people aware of Jesus' glory begin.

112   *LIFE IN THE SPIRIT*   □

I remember walking to church one winter evening to preach on the words, 'He will bring glory to me', seeing the building floodlit as I turned a corner, and realising that this was exactly the illustration my message needed. When floodlighting is well done, the floodlights are placed so that you do not see them; in fact, you are not supposed to see where the light is coming from; what you are meant to see is just the building on which the floodlights are trained. The intended effect is to make it visible when otherwise it would not be seen for the darkness, and to maximise its dignity by throwing all its details into relief so that you can see it properly. This perfectly illustrates the Spirit's new covenant role. He is, so to speak, the hidden floodlight shining on the Saviour.

Or think of it this way. It is as if the Spirit stands behind us, throwing light over our shoulder on to Jesus who stands facing us. The Spirit's message to us is never, 'Look at me; listen to me; come to me; get to know me,' but always, 'Look at him, and see his glory; listen to him and hear his word; go to him and have life; get to know him and taste his gift of joy and peace.'[1]

The Spirit, we might say, is the matchmaker, the celestial marriage broker, whose role it is to bring us and Christ together and ensure that we stay together, so that three things keep happening:

First, personal *fellowship* with Jesus (the to-and-fro of discipleship with devotion which started in Palestine for Jesus' first followers before his passion) becomes a reality of experience, even though Jesus is not here on earth in bodily form today but is enthroned in heaven's glory.

Second, *transformation* of character into Jesus' likeness starts to take place as, looking to Jesus as their model for strength, believers worship and adore him and learn to lay out and, indeed, lay down their lives for him and for others.

Third, the Spirit-given *certainty* of being loved, redeemed, and adopted through Christ into the Father's family, so as to be heirs of God and fellow heirs with Christ, makes gratitude, delight, hope, and confidence – in a word, *assurance* – blossom in believers' hearts. This is the proper way to understand many of the Christians' post-conversion mountaintop experiences. The inward coming of the Son and the Father that Jesus promised takes place through the Spirit and its effect is to intensify assurance.

By these phenomena of experience, Spirit-given knowledge of Christ's presence shows itself.[2]

Reflection

What aspect of Jesus' ministry do you feel you need the Holy Spirit to floodlight particularly for you at present?

Write a prayer asking him to do just that and pray it regularly. On the basis of 1 John 5:14, 15, can you expect it to be answered?

Lord I wish to serve you & be used by you. Show me how / where & give me courage & humility to obey.

27

Guidance and guidelines

Reading: Romans 8:5–10

Those who live according to the sinful nature have their minds set on what that nature desires; but those who live in accordance with the Spirit have their minds set on what the Spirit desires. The mind of sinful man is death, but the mind controlled by the Spirit is life and peace; the sinful mind is hostile to God. It does not submit to God's law, nor can it do so. Those controlled by the sinful nature cannot please God.

You, however, are controlled not by the sinful nature but by the Spirit, if the Spirit of God lives in you. And if anyone does not have the Spirit of Christ, he does not belong to Christ. But if Christ is in you, your body is dead because of sin, yet your spirit is alive because of righteousness.

If we want God to guide us, our attitude needs to be right. Here are some guidelines as to how we can play our part in arriving at right decisions.

First, we must be willing to *think*. It is false piety,

GUIDANCE AND GUIDELINES 115

super-supernaturalism of an unhealthy pernicious sort that demands inward impressions with no rational base, and declines to heed the constant biblical summons to consider. God made us thinking beings, and he guides our minds as we think things out in his presence.

Second, we must be willing to *think ahead* and weigh the long-term consequences of alternative courses of action. Often we can only see what is wise and right, and what is foolish and wrong, as we dwell on the long-term issues.

Third, we must be willing to *take advice*. It is a sign of conceit and immaturity to dispense with taking advice in major decisions. There are always people who know the Bible, human nature, and our own gifts and limitations better than we do, and even if we cannot finally accept their advice, nothing but good will come to us from carefully weighing what they say.

Fourth, we must be willing to *be ruthlessly honest with ourselves*. We must suspect ourselves: ask ourselves why we feel a particular course of action will be right and make ourselves give reasons.

Fifth, we must be willing to *wait*. 'Wait on the Lord' is a constant refrain in the Psalms and it is a necessary word, for the Lord often keeps us waiting. When in doubt, do nothing, but continue to wait on God.[1]

The basic form of divine guidance is the presentation of positive ideals as guidelines for all our living. 'Be the kind of person Jesus was'; 'seek this virtue and this one and practise them to the limit'; 'know your responsibilities – husbands, to your wives; wives, to your husbands; parents, to your children; all of you, to your fellow Christians and all your fellow-men; know them and seek strength constantly to discharge them': this is how God guides us through the Bible, as any student of the Psalms, the Proverbs, the prophets, the Sermon on the Mount, and the ethical parts of the epistles will soon discover. 'Turn from evil, and do good' – this is the highway along which the Bible leads us, and all its admonitions keep us on it. Being led by the Spirit relates not to inward voices or any such experiences, but to mortifying known sin and not living after the flesh!

Only within the limits of *this* guidance does God prompt us inwardly in matters of vocational decision. So never expect to be guided to marry an unbeliever, or elope with a married person. I have known divine guidance to be claimed for both courses of action. Inward inclinations were undoubtedly present, but they were quite certainly not from the Spirit of God, for they went against the Bible. The Spirit 'guides me in paths of righteousness' – but not anywhere else.[2]

Reflection

What have you felt guided to do in the past? What do you feel guided to do now or in the future?

Strike off whatever in the light of the above guidelines couldn't come under the heading of 'guided by the Spirit'.

GUIDANCE AND GUIDELINES 117

Are you willing (or willing to become willing) to submit to the Spirit and spiritual guidelines where you've been guided by some other agency or agenda? If so, tell God, and ask for his Spirit's help with any attitude change or action that may be necessary.

28

Spiritual authority

Reading: Acts 4:31-33

After they prayed, the place where they were meeting was shaken. And they were all filled with the Holy Spirit and spoke the word of God boldly.

All the believers were one in heart and mind. No one claimed that any of his possessions was his own, but they shared everything they had. With great power the apostles continued to testify to the resurrection of the Lord Jesus, and much grace was upon them all.

Jesus gave the Spirit to his people. In these days we need to remind ourselves of that. If we want the Spirit or more of the Spirit, we must seek Jesus who gives him.

The Spirit's first work is to bring the Lord's people into communion with their Saviour. 'He will bring glory to me by taking from what is mine and making it known to you' (John 16:14). He will 'teach you all things and will remind you of everything I have said to you' (John 14:26). In other words: He'll make fellowship between you and the Lord – you as the needy one and

SPIRITUAL AUTHORITY

the Lord as risen, triumphant, and living – a happy reality.

As a result of that will come boldness. 'They were all filled with the Holy Spirit and spoke the word of God boldly.' When the Spirit of Christ is revealing to the Christian just how rich he is in Christ and just how close Christ is to him, the inhibitions drop away, and the saint is able to speak boldly and feelingly of what God has done for him.

Something else which flows from this is discernment and authority. The people of God with the authority of Christ may and must tell the world that everyone who repents and trusts the Saviour will have his sins forgiven, and that until they do, there is no forgiveness for them. As counsellors and helpers, it's the privilege of all Christians to say to people who are genuinely repentant and genuinely believe in Jesus: 'I tell you that for Christ's sake your sins are forgiven.' On the other hand we may have to tell others that since they have not yet repented, their sins are retained. It is the Spirit who gives us the discernment to do this, as he did to Peter (see Acts 8:18–24), along with giving us the authority for doing it.[1]

The empowering from Christ through the Spirit is a momentous New Testament fact, one of the glories of the gospel and a mark of Christ's true followers everywhere. When the Spirit had been poured out at Pentecost, 'with great power the apostles continued to testify to the resurrection of the Lord Jesus'; 'and Stephen, a man full of grace and power, did great wonders and miraculous signs among the people'.

Paul prays for the Romans that by the power of the Holy Spirit they would abound in hope. Then he speaks of 'what Christ has accomplished through me . . . by what I have said and done, by the power of signs and miracles through the power of the Holy Spirit' (Rom. 15:18–19). He reminds the Corinthians that he preached Christ crucified in demonstration of the Spirit and power, that their faith might rest in the power of God.

He emphasises to Timothy that God has given Christians a spirit of power and of love and of self-control and censures those who are 'lovers of pleasure rather than lovers of God – having a form of godliness but denying its power' (2 Tim. 1:7; 3:4–5). There is no mistaking the thrust of all this. What we are being told is that supernatural living through supernatural empowering is at the very heart of New Testament Christianity, so that those who, while professing faith, do not show forth this empowering are suspect by New Testament standards. And the empowering is always the work of the Holy Spirit, even when Christ only is named as its source, for Christ is the Spirit giver.[2]

Reflection

Does the thought of wielding spiritual authority scare or thrill you? Why do you think this is? (Temperament? Offputting experiences? . . .)

Now, talk to God about your feelings and, with the biblical guidelines in mind, pray for spiritual authority and the wisdom to use it well.

For further study
Study the reading and also Acts 10:38; 2 Timothy 1:7 and 1 Corinthians 2:1–5. What do these passages say about spiritual power and authority: its source and what it is or is not dependent on; what it's for and what it needs to be tempered by?

29

Spiritual movements

Reading: Psalm 85:1–7

*You showed favour to your land, O Lord;
  you restored the fortunes of Jacob.
You forgave the iniquity of your people
  and covered all their sins.
You set aside all your wrath
  and turned from your fierce anger.
Restore us again, O God our Saviour,
  and put away your displeasure towards us.
Will you be angry with us for ever?
Will you prolong your anger
  through all generations?
Will you not revive us again,
  that your people may rejoice in you?
Show us your unfailing love, O Lord,
  and grant us your salvation.*

Renewal is a general experiential deepening of the life in the Spirit which is the foretaste and first instalment of heaven itself. Assurance of both the shameful guiltiness

SPIRITUAL MOVEMENTS

and the total pardon of our sins; humble but exalted joy in the awareness of God's love for us; knowledge of the closeness of the Father and the Son in both communion and affection; a never-ending passion to praise God; an abiding urge to love, serve, and honour the Father, the Son, the Spirit, and the saints, and the inward freedom to express that urge creatively and spontaneously – these things will be the essence of the life of heaven. They are already the leading marks of spiritually renewed individuals and communities in this world.

It is in renewal that love for Jesus and fellowship with him become most clear-sighted and deep. The most obvious evidence of this is the hymnology of renewal movements.

Through renewal, believers are drawn deeper into their baptismal life of dying with Christ in repentance and self-denial and rising with him into the new righteousness of combating sin and living in obedience to God.

Renewal takes place through the action of the Holy Spirit doing his New Covenant work of glorifying the glorified Christ before the eyes of the understanding of his disciples.

In renewal God's people experience the termination of the impotence, frustration, and barrenness which have been the tokens of divine displeasure at unfaithfulness. Joy replaces the distress which they felt at God's displeasure, and God's kingdom is extended through the impact of their revitalised lives (Ps. 85:4–6; Zech. 8:23).[1]

Revival is a visitation of God which brings to life Christians who have been sleeping and restores a deep sense of God's near presence and holiness. Thence springs a vivid sense of sin and a profound exercise of heart in repentance, praise, and love, with an evangelistic outflow.

Each revival movement has its own distinctive features, but the pattern is the same every time.

First *God comes*. On New Year's Eve 1739, John Wesley, George Whitefield, and some of their friends held a 'love feast' which became a watchnight of prayer to see the New Year in. At about 3 a.m., Wesley wrote, 'The power of God came mightily upon us, insomuch that many cried for exceeding joy, and many fell to the ground.' Revival always begins with a restoration of the sense of the closeness of the Holy One.

Second, *the gospel is loved* as never before. The sense of God's nearness creates an overwhelming awareness of one's own sins and sinfulness, and so the power of the cleansing blood of Christ is greatly appreciated.

Then *repentance deepens*. In the Ulster revival in the 1920s shipyard workers brought back so many stolen tools that new sheds had to be built to house the recovered property! Repentance results in restitution.

Finally, *the Spirit works fast*: godliness multiplies, Christians mature, converts appear. Paul was at Thessalonica for less than three weeks, but God worked quickly and Paul left a virile church behind him.[2]

Reflection

How do you honestly feel when you think of powerful spiritual movements like renewal and revival? Tell God about your feelings.

As well as our fears or other feelings, hindrances to renewal and revival may also include clericalism as a leadership style as against every-member ministry; formalism as a worship style as against everyone having a genuine desire to meet God; complacency as against an eagerness to grow in worship, faith, repentance, knowledge, holiness.

Regular prayer with others about these and other blockages could be the place to start making way for renewal or revival where you are.

30

All this and heaven too!

Readings: 1 Corinthians 2:9–13; Philippians 4:8

'*No eye has seen,
   no ear has heard,
no mind has conceived
   what God has prepared for those who love him.*'
  But God has revealed it to us by his Spirit.
  The Spirit searches all things, even the deep things of God. For who among men knows the thoughts of a man except the man's spirit within him? In the same way no one knows the thoughts of God except the Spirit of God. We have not received the Spirit of the world but the Spirit who is from God, that we may understand what God has freely given us. This is what we speak, not in words of human wisdom but in words taught by the Spirit, expressing spiritual truths in spiritual words.
  Whatever is true, whatever is noble, whatever is right, whatever is pure, whatever is lovely, whatever is admirable – if anything is excellent or praiseworthy – think about such things.

ALL THIS AND HEAVEN TOO! 127

The Holy Spirit makes us realise that as Christ on earth loved us and died for us, so in glory now he loves us and lives for us as the mediator whose endless life guarantees us endless glory with him. He also makes us see that through Christ, in Christ, and with Christ, we are now God's children; and hereby leads us spontaneously and instinctively – for there are spiritual instincts as well as natural ones – to think of God as Father and so to address him.

To know that God is your Father and that he loves you, his adopted child, no less than he loves his only-begotten Son, and that enjoyment of God's love and glory for all eternity is pledged to you bring inward delight that is sometimes overwhelming; and this is also the Spirit's doing.

Also, the Holy Spirit given to us is the 'first fruits' because by enabling us to see Christ glorified and to live in fellowship with him as our mediator and with his Father as our father, he introduces us to the inmost essence of the life of heaven. To think of heaven as a place and a state cannot be wrong, for the Bible writers do it; nonetheless what makes heaven *heaven* and what must always be at the heart of our thoughts about heaven is the actual relationship with the Father and the Son that is perfected there. This is the first instalment of the Spirit's present ministry to us.[1]

As I get older, I find that I appreciate God and people and good and lovely and noble things more and more intensely; so it is pure delight to think that this enjoyment will continue and increase in some form (what form, God knows, and I am content to wait and see), literally for ever. In fact Christians inherit the destiny which fairy tales envisaged in fancy: *we* (yes, you and I, the silly saved sinners) *live* and live *happily*, and by God's endless mercy will live happily *ever after*.

We cannot visualise heaven's life and the wise person will not try to do so. Instead he or she will dwell on the doctrine of heaven, where the redeemed will find all their heart's desire: joy with their Lord, joy with his people, and joy in the ending of all frustration and distress and in the supply of all wants. What was said to the child – 'If you want sweets and hamsters in heaven, they'll be there' – was not an evasion but a witness to the truth that in heaven no felt needs or longings go unsatisfied. What our wants will actually be, however, we hardly know, except the first and foremost: we shall want to be 'with the Lord for ever' (1 Thess. 4:17).

What shall we do in heaven? Not lounge around but worship, work, think, and communicate, enjoying activity, beauty, people, and God. First and foremost, however, we shall see and love Jesus, our Saviour, Master, and Friend.[2]

Reflection

How much does heaven fill your thoughts?

Should it be only when we become senior citizens that we reflect on our eternal future?

Spend some time thinking about heaven. Jot down the thoughts, feelings, images, which such reflection conjures up.

Turn these into a song, prayer or joyful thought for the day.

Notes

Throughout these Notes, the dates refer to extracts from *Through the Year with J. I. Packer* (Hodder and Stoughton, 1986); full details of the works mentioned will be found in the Bibliography.

Chapter 1

1. 10th May. 'Life in Christ'.
2. 22nd January. 'Regeneration'.

Chapter 2

1. 28th January. *Keep in Step with the Spirit*.
2. 7th August. 'Predestination and Sanctification'.

Chapter 3

1. 10th January. 'The Way of Salvation'.
2. 22nd May. Taped message.

Chapter 4

1. 13th July. 'Joy'.
2. 14th July. 'Joy'.

Chapter 5

1. 11th December. *We Believe*.
2. 24th January. *Keep in Step with the Spirit*.

Chapter 6

1. 21st January. Taped message.
2. 6th November. *Knowing God*.

Chapter 7

1. 12th September. *Keep in Step with the Spirit*.
2. 10th March. 'Life in Christ'.

Chapter 8

1. 26th November. 'The Holy Spirit and the Local Congregation'.
2. 3rd March. 'Training for Christian Service'.

Chapter 9

1. 16th March. Taped message.
2. 24th May. Taped message.

Chapter 10

1. 30th November. 'The Nature of the Church'.
2. 17th September. *Keep in Step with the Spirit*.

Chapter 11

1. 9th February. *Keep in Step with the Spirit*.
2. 28th April. *Beyond the Battle for the Bible*.

Chapter 12

1. 15th June. *We Believe*.
2. 13th February. 'A Lamp in a Dark Place'.

Chapter 13

1. 16th June. *God Has Spoken*.
2. 8th February. 'Knowing Notions or Knowing God?'

Chapter 14

1. 10th November. *God Has Spoken*.
2. 29th April. *Beyond the Battle for the Bible*.

Chapter 15

1. 27th May. Taped message.
2. 16th February. *Keep in Step with the Spirit*.

Chapter 16

1. 29th January. *Keep in Step with the Spirit*.
2. 24th August. 'Life in Christ'.

Chapter 17

1. 31st October. Taped message.
2. 30th December. Taped message.

Chapter 18

1. 7th June. 'My Path of Prayer'.
2. 18th July. 'Life in Christ'.

Chapter 19

1. 3rd June. 'My Path of Prayer'.
2. 6th June. 'Life in Christ'.

Chapter 20

1. 1st June. Taped message.
2. 20th July. 'My Path of Prayer'.

Chapter 21

1. 2nd May. *We Believe*.
2. 15th July. *Tomorrow's Worship*.
3. William Temple, *Readings in St John's Gospel*, Macmillan, 1939, p. 68.

Chapter 22

1. 22nd November. 'Body Life'.
2. 12th March. *I Want to Be a Christian*.

Chapter 23

1. 14th September. 'Body Life'.
2. 5th March. 'Life in Christ'.

Chapter 24

1. 26th May. 'Body Life'.
2. 25th May. 'The Holy Spirit and the Local Congregation'.

Chapter 25

1. 9th April. *Keep in Step with the Spirit*.
2. 18th January. 'Life in Christ'.

Chapter 26

1. 1st February. *Keep in Step with the Spirit*.
2. 26th January. *Keep in Step with the Spirit*.

Chapter 27

1. 13th October. *Knowing God*.
2. 4th February. *Knowing God*.

Chapter 28

1. 30th January. Taped message.
2. 25th January. *Keep in Step with the Spirit*.

Chapter 29

1. 28th May. 'Steps to the Renewal of the Christian People'.
2. 30th May. 'Lord, Send Revival'.

Chapter 30

1. 27th January. *Keep in Step with the Spirit*.
2. 14th May. *I Want to Be a Christian*.

Bibliography

'A Lamp in a Dark Place' in *Can We Trust the Bible?*, ed. Earl Radmacher, Wheaton, Illinois: Tyndale House Publishers, 1979.

Beyond the Battle for the Bible, Westchester, Illinois: Good News Publishers/Crossway Books, 1980.

'Body Life' in *Tenth* (July 1981), Philadelphia: 10th Presbyterian Church, 1981.

God Has Spoken, Downers Grove, Illinois: InterVarsity Press, 1979.

I Want to Be a Christian, Wheaton, Illinois: Tyndale House Publishers, Inc., 1977.

'Joy' in *Discovery Papers*, (20th February 1977), Palo Alto, California: Peninsula Bible Church, 1977.

Keep in Step with the Spirit, Old Tappan, New Jersey: Fleming H. Revell Company, 1984.

Knowing God, Downers Grove, Illinois: InterVarsity Press, 1973.

'Knowing Notions or Knowing God?' in *Pastoral Renewal*, 6.9 (March 1982), Ann Arbor, Michigan: Pastoral Renewal, 1982.

'Life in Christ' in *Bible Characters and Doctrines*, Vol II, London, England: Scripture Union, 1974.

136 LIFE IN THE SPIRIT □

'Lord, Send Revival' in *The Bulletin of Westminster Theological Seminary* (Winter 1983), Philadelphia: Westminster Theological Seminary, 1983.

'My Path of Prayer' in *My Path of Prayer*, ed. David Hanes, Sussex, England: Henry E. Walter Ltd, 1981.

'Predestination and Sanctification' in *Tenth* (July 1983), Philadelphia: 10th Presbyterian Church, 1983.

'Regeneration' in *Baker's Dictionary of Theology*, ed. C. F. H. Henry, Grand Rapids, Michigan: Baker Book House, 1959; Rev. to *Evangelical Dictionary of Theology*, ed. Walter Elwell, Grand Rapids, Michigan: Baker Book House, 1984.

'Steps to the Renewal of the Christian People' in *Summons to Faith and Renewal in a Post-Christian World*, ed. Peter Williamson and Kevin Perrotta, Ann Arbor, Michigan: Servant Publications, 1983.

'The Holy Spirit and the Local Congregation' in *Churchman* LXXVIII.2 (June 1964), London, England: Church Society, 1964.

'The Nature of the Church' in *Basic Christian Doctrines*, ed. C. F. H. Henry, New York: Holt, Rinehart & Winston, 1962.

'The Way of Salvation' in *Bibliotheca Sacra* nos 515–18 (Part 1, July 1972–April 1973), Dallas, Texas: Dallas Theological Seminary, 1972.

Tomorrow's Worship, London, England: Church Book Room Press, 1966.

'Training for Christian Service' in the *Evangelical Christian* (September 1961), Toronto, Ontario: Evangelical Publishers, 1961.

We Believe, Surrey, England: The Nurses Christian Fellowship, 1972.

FOR FURTHER NOTES

LIFE IN THE SPIRIT

FOR FURTHER NOTES

140   LIFE IN THE SPIRIT

Seeking the Kingdom

Another title from the *20 Minutes with God* series

A major new list of exciting spiritual devotions written by popular Christian authors.

Seeking the Kimgdom starts by looking inward to focus the heart on God, then moves upward to develop an intimacy with God, and finally travels outward to bring God to others.

It includes thirty guided devotions that are ideal for daily use or for prayer partners and fellowship groups. Each meditation opens with a short passage of Scripture followed by a helpful comment or insight from Richard Foster. Within each 20 minutes there is also time for reflection and some simple spiritual exercises.

Richard Foster, a Quaker, is the author of many best-selling books including *Prayer* and *Celebration of Discipline*. He is Professor of Spiritual Formation at Azusa Pacific University, USA.

Richard Foster
(ISBN 0 340 64262 9)

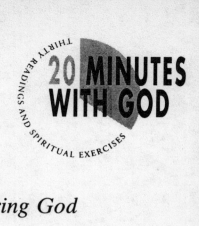

Encountering God

Another title from the *20 Minutes with God* series

A major new list of exciting spiritual devotions written by popular Christian authors.

In *Encountering God* Joyce Huggett explores how the Holy Spirit can transform our experience of daily life. In times of joy and pain, pressure and rest – God Himself can still be found.

It includes thirty guided devotions that are ideal for daily use or for prayer partners and fellowship groups. Each meditation opens with a short passage of Scripture followed by a helpful comment or insight from Joyce Huggett. Within each 20 minutes there is also time for reflection and some simple spiritual exercises.

Joyce Huggett is a mission partner with Interserve and lives with her husband David in Cyprus. She is a popular speaker and author of *Listening to God* and *Listening to Others*.

Joyce Huggett
(ISBN 0 340 64263 7)

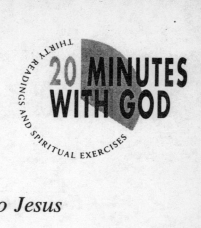

Closer to Jesus

Another title from the *20 Minutes with God* series

A major new list of exciting spiritual devotions written by popular Christian authors.

Experiencing the presence of Jesus is the theme for this book. Sitting at His feet through times of joy, failure, doubt and triumph, we are transformed by the power of his love.

It includes thirty guided devotions that are ideal for daily use or for prayer partners and fellowship groups. Each meditation opens with a short passage of Scripture followed by a helpful comment or insight from J. L. Packer. Within each 20 minutes there is also time for reflection and some simple spiritual exercises.

Canon Michael Green is Adviser in Evangelism to the Archbishops of Canterbury and York and joint co-ordinator of the Springboard initiative for the Decade of Evangelism.

Michael Green
(ISBN 0 340 64217 3)